THE BROTHERS LIONHEART
BY ASTRID LINDGREN
Drawings by J. K. Lambert

"Now I'm going to tell you about my brother, Jonathan. I think it's almost like a saga, and just a little like a ghost story, and yet every word is true, though Jonathan and I are probably the only people who know that."

When Karl and Jonathan Lionheart arrive in the kingdom of Nangiyala, they find a beautiful medieval land where the people live a simple, pastoral life and the brothers can find the peace they never had in their own world. But that hope is shattered by news from Karmanyaka, the country across the Ancient Mountains: the cruel tyrant Lord Tengil has tightened his rule, keeping the citizens in constant fear with his savage army and the vicious dragon Katla. And now Tengil even threatens to cross the mountains to take control of Nangiyala.

Now Jonathan must go to join the secret struggle against Tengil, leaving his beloved brother behind. But when Karl hears that Jonathan is in mortal danger, he realizes that he must forget his past fears and join Jonathan in the battle across the mountains.

ALSO BY ASTRID LINDGREN

The Brothers Lionheart

ASTRID LINDGREN

Translated by Joan Tate

Drawings by J. K. Lambert

Puffin Books

PUFFIN BOOKS

Published by the Penguin Group
Penguin Books Ltd, 27 Wrights Lane, London W8 5TZ, England
Penguin Putnam Inc., 375 Hudson Street, New York, New York 10014, USA
Penguin Books Australia Ltd, Ringwood, Victoria, Australia
Penguin Books Canada Ltd, 10 Alcorn Avenue, Toronto, Ontario, Canada M4V 3B2
Penguin Books (NZ) Ltd, Private Bag 102902, NSMC, Auckland, New Zealand

On the World Wide Web at: www.penguin.com

Penguin Books Ltd, Registered Offices: Harmondsworth, Middlesex, England

First published in Swedish under the title *Bröderna Lejonhjärta* by Rabén Sjögren 1973
This English translation first published in Great Britain by Brockhampton Press Ltd 1975
Published in Puffin Books 1985
Reissued in this edition 2000

1

Text copyright © Astrid Lindgren, 1973
English translation copyright © Brockhampton Press Ltd, 1975
Illustrations copyright ©The Viking Press, Inc., 1975
All rights reserved

Filmset in Cloister Medium

Made and printed in England by Clays Ltd, St Ives plc

British Library Cataloguing in Publication Data
A CIP catalogue record for this book is available from the British Library

ISBN 0–141–31081–2

CHAPTER ONE

NOW I'M GOING TO TELL YOU ABOUT MY
brother. My brother, Jonathan Lionheart, is the person I
want to tell you about. I think it's almost like a saga, and just a
little like a ghost story, and yet every word is true, though
Jonathan and I are probably the only people who know that.

Jonathan's name wasn't Lionheart from the start. His last
name was Lion, just like Mother's and mine. Jonathan Lion
was his name. My name is Karl Lion and Mother's is Sigrid
Lion. Father was called Axel Lion, but he went to sea and we
have never heard from him since.

But what I was going to tell you was how it came about
that my brother Jonathan became Jonathan Lionheart, and all
the strange things that happened after that.

Jonathan knew that I was soon going to die. I think everyone knew except me. They knew at school too, because I was
away most of the time, coughing and always being ill. For the
last six months, I haven't been able to go to school at all. All

7

the ladies Mother sews dresses for knew it too, and one of them was talking to Mother about it when I happened to hear, although I wasn't meant to. They thought I was asleep. But I was just lying there with my eyes closed. And I went on lying there like that, because I didn't want them to see that I had heard that terrible thing—that I was soon going to die.

I was sad, of course, and terribly afraid, and I didn't want Mother to see that. But I talked to Jonathan about it when he came home.

"Did you know that I'm going to die?" I said, and I wept.

Jonathan thought for a moment. Perhaps he didn't really want to answer, but in the end he said:

"Yes, I know."

Then I cried even more.

"How can things be so terrible?" I asked. "How can things be so terrible that some people have to die, when they're not even ten years old?"

"You know, Rusky, I don't think it's that terrible," said Jonathan. "I think you'll have a marvelous time."

"Marvelous," I said. "Is it marvelous to lie under the ground and be dead?"

"Oh," said Jonathan. "It's only your shell that lies there, you know? You yourself fly away somewhere quite different."

"Where?" I asked, because I could hardly believe him.

"To Nangiyala," he said.

To Nangiyala—he just threw out the word as if it were something everyone in the world knew. But at the time, I had never heard it mentioned before.

"Nangiyala?" I said. "Where's that?"

Then Jonathan said that he wasn't quite certain, but it was somewhere on the other side of the stars. And he began to tell me about Nangiyala, so that I almost felt like flying there at once.

"It's still in the days of campfires and sagas there," he said, "and you'll like that."

All the sagas came from Nangiyala, he said, for it was there that everything of that kind happened, and if you went there, then you could take part in adventures from morning till evening, and at night too, Jonathan said.

"You know, Rusky," he said, "that'll be different from lying here and coughing and being ill and never able to play, won't it?"

Jonathan always called me Rusky. He'd done that ever since I was small, and when I asked him why once, he said it was because he liked rusks so much, especially rusks like me. Yes, he liked me, Jonathan, and that was strange, for I've never been anything but a rather ugly, stupid, and cowardly boy, with crooked legs and all. I asked Jonathan how he could like such an ugly, stupid boy like me, with crooked legs and all, and then he said:

"If you weren't such a nice, ugly little paleface with crooked legs, then you wouldn't be my Rusky, the one I like."

But that evening, when I was so afraid of dying, he said that as long as I got to Nangiyala, then I would at once be well and strong and even beautiful, too.

"As beautiful as you?" I asked.

"Much more beautiful," said Jonathan.

But he shouldn't have tried that on me, because there's never been anything so beautiful as Jonathan and there never will be.

Once, one of those ladies Mother sews for said:

"My dear Mrs. Lion, you've got a son who looks like a prince in a saga."

And she wasn't talking about me, either!

Jonathan really did look like a prince in a saga. His hair shone like gold and he had beautiful dark-blue eyes which really shone, and beautiful white teeth and perfectly straight legs.

And not only that. He was kind and strong, and he knew everything and understood everything and was tops in school, and all the children in the yard hung around him wherever he went, wanting to be with him, and he found amusing things for them and took them on adventures, and I could never go with them, because I was lying on my old kitchen sofa-bed day in and day out. But Jonathan told me everything when he came home, everything he'd been doing and everything he'd seen and heard and read. He would sit for ages on the edge of my bed and tell me. Jonathan slept in the kitchen, too, in a bed which he had to get out of the clothes closet in the evenings. And when he had gone to bed, he went on telling me stories and sagas, until Mother called in from the other room:

"You two must be quiet now. Kalle must sleep."

But it is difficult to sleep when you are coughing all the time. Sometimes, Jonathan got up in the middle of the night and boiled honey water for me to soothe my cough. He was kind, Jonathan was.

That evening, when I was so afraid of dying, he sat with me for several hours and we talked about Nangiyala, but very quietly so that Mother wouldn't hear. She was sitting sewing as usual, but she has her sewing machine in her room, the room where she sleeps—we only have one room and the kitchen, you see. The door into her room was open, and we could hear her singing that old song about a seaman far away at sea; it was Father she was thinking about, I suppose. I don't remember very well how it goes. I only remember a few lines which go like this:

> If I die at sea, dear,
> perhaps there'll be a day
> when a snow-white pigeon comes
> from far, far away;

> *then hasten to the sill, dear,*
> *it's my soul that's there,*
> *wanting to rest a while, here*
> *in your arms so dear.*

It is a beautiful and sad song, I think, but Jonathan laughed when he heard it and said:

"You know, Rusky, perhaps you'll come flying to me one evening. From Nangiyala. And please don't forget to sit there like a snow-white pigeon on the windowsill, will you?"

I began to cough then, and he lifted me up and held me in his arms as he usually did when it was worst, and he sang:

> *My little Rusky, I know, dear*
> *that your soul is here*
> *wanting to rest a while here*
> *in my arms so dear.*

Not until then did I begin to think about what it would be like in Nangiyala without Jonathan. How lonely I would be without him! What good would it be to be where there were lots and lots of sagas and adventures if Jonathan were not there too? I would just be afraid and not know what to do.

"I don't want to go there," I said, and I wept. "I want to be where you are, Jonathan."

"But I'm coming to Nangiyala, too, don't you see?" said Jonathan. "After a while."

"After a while, yes," I said. "But perhaps you'll live until you're ninety years old, and in the meantime I'll be there alone."

Then Jonathan said that there was no *time* in Nangiyala the way it is on earth. Even if he did live until he was ninety, it wouldn't seem like more than two days at the most before he came. That's what it's like when there isn't any real time.

"You could manage on your own for two days, couldn't you?" he said. "You could climb the trees and make a campfire in the forest and sit by a small stream and fish, all those things you've longed to do so much. And just as you're sitting there, catching a perch, I'll come flying in and you'll say, 'Good heavens, Jonathan, are you here already?'"

I tried to stop crying, because I thought I might be able to last out those two days.

"Just think how good it would be if you'd gone there first," I said, "so that it was you who was sitting there fishing."

Jonathan agreed with me. He looked at me for a long time, kindly as usual, and I noticed he was sad, because he said very quietly and rather sorrowfully:

"But instead I'll have to live on earth without my Rusky. For ninety years, perhaps!"

That's what we thought!

CHAPTER TWO

NOW I'M COMING TO THE DIFFICULT PART, the part I can't bear thinking about, the part I can't help thinking about.

My brother Jonathan; it might have been that he was still with me, sitting talking to me in the evenings, going to school and playing with the kids in the yard and boiling honey water for me and all that. But it isn't like that . . . it *isn't*.

Jonathan is in Nangiyala now.

It's difficult, I can't, now—I *can't* tell you. But this is what it said in the paper afterwards:

> *A terrible fire swept through the Fackelrosen building here in town last night. One of the old wooden buildings was burned to the ground and a life was lost.*
>
> *A ten-year-old boy, Karl Lion, was alone when the fire broke out, lying ill in a second-floor apartment. Soon after the outbreak, his brother, thirteen-year-old Jonathan Lion,*

returned home, and before anyone could stop him, he had rushed into the blazing building to rescue his brother. Within seconds, however, the whole of the staircase was a sea of flames, and there was nothing to do but for the two boys trapped by the flames to try to save themselves by jumping out of the window. The horrified crowd that had gathered outside was forced to witness how the thirteen-year-old unhesitatingly took his brother on his back, and with the fire roaring behind him, threw himself out of the window. In his fall to the ground, the boy was injured so badly that he died almost instantaneously. The younger brother, on the other hand, protected by his brother's body in the fall, was uninjured.

The mother of the two boys was on a visit to a customer at the time—she is a dressmaker—and she received a severe shock on her arrival home. It is not known how the fire started.

On another page of the newspaper, there was more about Jonathan, which the schoolteacher had written.
This is what it said:

Jonathan Lion dear, shouldn't your name really have been Jonathan Lionheart? Do you remember when we read in the history book about a brave young English king whose name was Richard the Lionheart? Do you remember how you said, "Just think of being so brave that they write about it in the history books afterward; I'd never be like that!" Dear Jonathan, even if they don't write about you in the history books, you were just as brave at the critical moment and you were a hero as great as any other. Your old schoolteacher will never forget you. Your friends will

*also remember you for a long time. It will be empty in the
classroom without our happy and beautiful Jonathan. But
the gods love those who die young. Rest in Peace, Jonathan
Lionheart.*

GRETA ANDERSSON

She's pretty silly, Jonathan's schoolteacher, but she liked
Jonathan very much, just as everyone else did, and it was good
that she thought up that business about Lionheart. That was
really good.

There probably isn't a single person in town who doesn't
grieve for Jonathan, or who doesn't think it would have been
better if I had died instead. At least, that's what I gather from
all the women who come here with their materials and muslins
and stuff. They sigh and look at me when they go through the
kitchen, and they say to Mother, "Poor Mrs. Lion! And
Jonathan too, who was so exceptional."

We live in the building next door to our old building now,
in an apartment exactly like the old one, but it's on the ground
floor. We have been given some second-hand furniture by the
parish, and the women have also given us some things. I lie
in a sofa-bed almost identical to my old one. Everything is
almost like it was before. And yet everything—absolutely
everything—is not like it was before. For there's no Jonathan
any longer. No one sits with me and tells me things in the
evenings. I'm so lonely that it hurts inside me and all I can do
is to lie and whisper to myself the words that Jonathan said
just before he died, that moment when we were lying on the
ground after we had jumped. He was lying face down, of course,
but someone turned him over and I saw his face. A little blood
was running out of the corner of his mouth and he could hardly
speak. But it was as if he were trying to smile all the same, and

he managed a few words. "Don't cry, Rusky. We'll meet in Nangiyala."

He said just that and nothing more. Then he closed his eyes and people came and took him away, and I never saw him again.

I don't want to remember the time just afterward. But you can't forget anything so terrible and painful. I lay here in my sofa-bed and thought about Jonathan until I thought my head would burst, and no one could possibly long for someone as I longed for him. I was frightened, too. I kept thinking, suppose all that about Nangiyala wasn't true, suppose it was just one of those things that Jonathan used to think up? I cried and cried.

But then Jonathan came and comforted me. Yes, he came and oh, it was marvelous. Everything was almost all right again. He probably knew over there in Nangiyala what it was like for me without him and thought he ought to come and comfort me. So he came to me and now I'm not so sad any longer; now I'm just waiting.

It was one evening a little while ago that he came. I was alone at home and I was lying in bed crying for him and I was more frightened and unhappy and ill and wretched than I can say. The kitchen window was open because it's fine warm spring weather now. I heard the pigeons cooing out there. There are lots of them here in the backyard and they coo all the time in the spring.

Then it happened.

Just as I'm lying there crying into my pillow, I hear a cooing quite close to me, and when I look up, there's a pigeon sitting on the windowsill, looking at me with kind eyes. A *snow-white* pigeon, please note, not one of those gray ones like the ones in the yard. A snow-white pigeon; no one can imagine how I felt when I saw it, for it was just like in the song—"when a snow-white pigeon comes." And it was as if I heard Jonathan

17

singing all over again: "my little Rusky, I know, dear, that your soul is here," but now it was he who had come to me instead.

I wanted to say something but I couldn't. I just lay there and listened to the pigeon cooing, and behind its cooing, or in the middle of its cooing—or how shall I put it?—I heard Jonathan's voice, though it didn't sound as it usually did. It was just like whispering all over the kitchen. Perhaps this sounds a bit like a ghost story, and perhaps I should have been frightened but I wasn't. I was just so happy, I could have jumped up to the ceiling, for everything that I heard was marvelous.

Then it was true, all that about Nangiyala. Jonathan wanted me to hurry there, because everything there was good in every way, he said. Just think, there was a house waiting for him when he arrived; he had been given a house all his own in Nangiyala. It's an old farm, he said, called Knights Farm, and it's in Cherry Valley. Doesn't that sound wonderful? And, just think, the first thing he saw when he got to Knights Farm was a little green notice on the gate, and on that notice was painted: THE LIONHEART BROTHERS.

"Which means we're both to live there," said Jonathan.

Just think, I too will be called Lionheart, *me*, when I get to Nangiyala. I'm glad about that, because I'd prefer to have the same name as Jonathan, even if I'm not so brave as he is.

"Come as quickly as you can," he said. "If you can't find me at Knights Farm, I'll be sitting fishing down by the stream."

Then it was quiet and the pigeon flew away, right over the roofs and back to Nangiyala.

And now I'm lying here on my sofa, just waiting to fly after it. I hope it's not too difficult to find my way there. But Jonathan said it wasn't at all difficult. I've written down the address, just to be sure: The Lionheart Brothers, Knights Farm, Cherry Valley, Nangiyala.

Jonathan has lived there alone for two months now. For two long, terrible months, I've had to be without him. But now I'm soon going to Nangilaya. Soon, soon, I'll be flying there. It feels as if it's going to be tonight. I'll write a note and put it on the kitchen table so that Mother finds it when she wakes up tomorrow morning:

Don't cry, Mother. See you in Nangiyala.

CHAPTER THREE

T HEN IT HAPPENED. AND I'VE NEVER BEEN
in on anything so strange. Suddenly I was standing in front
of the gate, reading that green notice: THE LIONHEART
BROTHERS.

How did I get there? When did I fly? How could I find my
way without asking anyone? I don't know. The only thing I
know is that suddenly I was standing there, looking at the
name on the gate.

I called to Jonathan. I called several times, but he didn't
answer, and then I remembered—of course, he was sitting
fishing down by the stream.

I started to run down the narrow path to the stream. I ran
and ran—and down there by the bridge was Jonathan. And
if I tell you this, I still can't tell you what it felt like to see
him again.

He didn't see me coming. I tried to call "Jonathan," but I
think I was crying, since nothing came out except a funny little

noise. But Jonathan heard it. He looked up and saw me. Then he cried out and flung down his fishing rod and rushed up to me and hugged me, just as if he wanted to feel that I had really come. Then I cried just a little. Why I should be crying, I don't know, but I had longed for him so much.

Jonathan laughed instead, and we stood there on the slope and hugged each other and were happier than I can say, because we were together again.

And then Jonathan said:

"Oh, so you've come at last, have you, Rusky Lionheart!"

Rusky Lionheart—it sounded crazy, so we giggled. And then we laughed more and more, just as if it were the funniest thing we'd heard for ages, though it was probably because we *wanted* something to laugh at. We were so happy that everything was whirling inside us. And when we'd laughed for ages, we wrestled together, but that didn't stop our laughing. No, indeed not; we went on until we fell over in the grass and we lay there and rolled around laughing more and more, finally laughing so much that we fell into the stream, and then we laughed so much that I thought we'd drown.

But instead we started to swim. I've never been able to swim, although I've always wanted to learn. Now I could, just like that. I was swimming away like anything.

"Jonathan, I can swim!" I shouted.

"Yes, of course you can swim," said Jonathan.

And then I suddenly thought of something.

"Jonathan, have you noticed something?" I said. "I've stopped coughing."

"Yes, of course you've stopped coughing," said Jonathan. "You're in Nangiyala now."

I swam around for quite a while and then I scrambled up on to the bridge and stood there, wet through, the water running out of my clothes. My trousers were clinging to my legs, which was why I could see so clearly what had happened. Believe it or not, my legs were quite straight, just like Jonathan's.

Then I thought, suppose I've become beautiful too? I asked Jonathan if he thought so, whether he could see if I had grown beautiful.

"Look in the mirror," he said, and he meant the stream, for the water was shiny and still, so that you could see your reflection in it. I lay down on my stomach on the bridge and peered over the edge and I saw myself in the water, but I didn't see anything particularly beautiful about me. Jonathan came and lay down beside me, and we lay there for a long time, peering at the Lionheart Brothers down there in the water, Jonathan so beautiful with his golden hair and his eyes and that fine face he has, and then me with my knobbly snout and straggly hair and all that.

"No, I don't think I've grown any more beautiful," I said.

But Jonathan thought there was a great difference now.

"And you look so healthy, too," he said.

Then I felt myself all over. I felt, as I lay there on the bridge, that I was healthy and well in every bit of me, so why did I need to be beautiful? My whole body was so happy that it seemed to be laughing all over.

We lay there for a while and let the sunlight warm us, and we watched the fish swimming in and out under the bridge. But then Jonathan wanted us to go home and so did I, because I was curious to see Knights Farm, where I was going to live.

Jonathan walked ahead of me up the path to the farm, and I trotted after him with my fine straight legs. I just walked along staring at my legs and feeling how good it was to walk with them. But when we'd got a little way up the slope, I suddenly turned my head. And then—then I saw Cherry Valley at last! Oh, that valley was white with cherry blossoms everywhere. White and green, it was, with cherry blossoms and green, green grass. And through all that green and white, the river flowed like a silver ribbon. Why hadn't I even noticed it before? Had I seen nothing but Jonathan? But now I stood quite still on the path and saw how beautiful it was, and I said to Jonathan:

"This must be the most beautiful valley on earth."

"Yes, but not on earth," said Jonathan, and then I remembered that I was in Nangiyala.

All around Cherry Valley were high mountains, and that was beautiful too. And down the mountain slopes, streams and waterfalls ran into the valley so that it sang of it, for it was spring.

There was something special about the air, too. It felt as if you could drink it, it was so pure and clean.

"They could do with a few kilos of this air back home," I said, as I remembered how I used to long for air as I lay on my kitchen sofa-bed, feeling as if there were no air at all.

But here there was, and I breathed in as much of it as I could. It was as if I couldn't have enough of it. Jonathan laughed at me and said:

"You might leave a little for me, you know."

The path we were on was white with fallen cherry blossoms, and fine white petals came whirling down on us, so that we got them in our hair and everywhere, but I like small green paths with cherry blossom petals on them, I really do.

And at the end of the path lay Knights Farm with the green notice on the gate.

"The Lionheart Brothers," I read aloud to Jonathan. "Just think this is where we're going to live."

"Yes, think of that, Rusky," said Jonathan. "Isn't it fine?"

And it was fine. I understood why Jonathan thought so. For my part, I couldn't even imagine anywhere better to live.

An old white house, not at all big, with green timbers and a green door and a bit of green ground all around, where cowslips and saxifrage and daisies grew in the grass. Lilacs and cherry trees too, in full bloom, and around it all was a stone wall, a little gray wall with pink flowers on it. You could have jumped over it easily, but nevertheless, once inside the gate, that wall felt as if it protected you from everything outside; it felt as if then you were home and on your own.

Actually there were two houses there, not just one, though the other one was more like a stable or something like that. They lay at an angle to each other, and just where they met was an old bench that looked as if it had come from the Stone Age, almost. It was a nice bench and a nice corner, anyhow. You almost felt like sitting there and thinking a little, or talking and looking at the birds and perhaps drinking fruit juice or something.

"I like it here," I said to Jonathan. "Is it just as nice indoors?"

"Come and look," he said. He was already standing by the door and just about to go in, but at that moment there was a whinny—yes, it really was a horse whinnying—and Jonathan said:

"I think we'll take the stable first."

He went into that other house and I ran after him; just you guess whether I ran after him!

It was indeed a stable, just as I'd thought, and there were two horses there, two beautiful brown horses, which turned their heads and whinnied at us as we came in through the door.

"This is Grim and Fyalar," said Jonathan. "Guess which is yours."

"Oh, go on," I said. "Don't you try telling me there's a horse for me, because I just don't believe it."

24

But Jonathan said that in Nangiyala no one could manage without a horse.

"You can't get anywhere without a horse," he said. "And you see, Rusky, you have to go a long way here sometimes."

It was the best thing I'd heard for ages—that you had to have a horse in Nangiyala—because I like horses so much. Think how soft their noses are. I don't think there's anything in the world so soft.

A pair of unusually beautiful horses they were, those two in the stable. Fyalar had a white blaze on his forehead, but otherwise they were just like each other.

"Then perhaps Grim is mine," I said. Jonathan wanted me to guess.

"Well, you're wrong there," said Jonathan. "Fyalar's yours."

I let Fyalar nuzzle me, and I patted him without being a bit scared, although I'd hardly ever touched a horse before. I liked him from the start, and he seemed to like me too, at least so I thought.

"We've got rabbits, too," said Jonathan. "In a hutch behind the stable. But you can look at them later."

I might have guessed it!

"I *must* see them now, at once," I said, for I've always wanted to keep rabbits and at home in town you just couldn't have them.

I made a quick little tour around behind the stable, and there in a hutch were indeed three lovely little rabbits, chewing on some dandelion leaves.

"It's funny," I said to Jonathan afterward. "Here in Nangiyala there's everything I ever wished for."

"Yes, but that's what I told you," said Jonathan. And it really was exactly as he'd told me, while he'd sat there with me in the kitchen at home. Though now I was able to see that it was true, too, and I was pleased about that.

There are some things you never forget. Never, ever, shall I forget that first evening in the kitchen at Knights Farm, how wonderful it was and what it felt like to lie talking to Jonathan just as before. Now we were living in a kitchen again as we had always done, although it didn't look like our kitchen at home in town, that's for sure. The kitchen at Knights Farm must be ancient, I thought, with its thick beams in the ceiling and its large open fireplace. What a fireplace: it took up half the wall and if you wanted to cook some food, you had to do it directly over the fire, just as they used to in the old days. In the middle of the floor was the sturdiest table I've ever seen in my life, with long, wooden benches down each side, and I reckon at least a score of people could sit there and eat at the same time without being too crowded.

"We might as well live in the kitchen as we used to," said Jonathan. "Then Mother can have the other room when she comes."

One room and a kitchen, that was what Knights Farm was, but we weren't used to and didn't need any more. All the same, it was at least twice as big as at home.

At home! I told Jonathan about the note I had left on the kitchen table for Mother.

"I wrote to her that we'd meet in Nangiyala. Though who knows when she'll come."

"It may be some time," said Jonathan. "But she'll have a good room with space for ten sewing machines, if she wants them."

Guess what I like! I like lying in an ancient old cupboard-bed in an ancient old kitchen, talking to Jonathan while the light from the fire flickers around the walls, and when I look out of the window, I see a branch of a cherry tree swaying in the evening breeze. And then the fire gets smaller and smaller, until only the embers are left, and the shadows thicken in the corners, and I get sleepier and sleepier, and I lie there and don't cough and Jonathan tells me things. Tells me and tells me and tells me, and in the end I hear his voice just like those whisperings again, and then I fall asleep. That's exactly what I like, and that's what it was like that first evening at Knights Farm, and that's why I'll never forget it.

CHAPTER FOUR

AND THE NEXT MORNING WE WENT RIDING.
Oh, yes, I *could* ride, and yet it was the first time I'd ever
been on horseback—I can't understand how things are like that
in Nangiyala, that you can do just anything, I mean. I galloped
on as if I'd never done anything else.

But Jonathan when he was riding! The woman who had
thought that my brother looked like a prince in a saga, she
should have been there as he came swooping along on his horse
through the meadows in Cherry Valley, then she would have
seen a saga prince that she never would have forgotten! Oh, as
he came at a gallop and then leapt over the stream, as if flying,
so that his hair was flowing around him, yes, you really could believe that he was a prince in a saga. He was nearly always
dressed like that, or perhaps more like a knight. There were lots
of clothes in a cupboard at Knights Farm, wherever they had
come from, and they weren't anything like the clothes we have
nowadays, but just like a knight's clothes. We had taken some
out for me, too, having thrown away my ugly old rags, which

28

I never wanted to see again. For Jonathan said we must be dressed so that it suited the times we were living in now; otherwise the people in Cherry Valley would think we were peculiar. The days of campfires and sagas: wasn't that what Jonathan had said? As we were riding around in that beautiful valley of ours, I asked him:

"They must be dreadfully olden days that we're living in here in Nangiyala, mustn't they?"

"You could say that, in some ways," said Jonathan. "They're olden days for us. But you could also say that they were young days."

He thought for a while.

"Yes, that's it," he said. "Young, healthy, and good days, which are easy and simple to live in."

But then his eyes darkened.

"At least, here in Cherry Valley," he said.

"Is it different in other places?" I asked, and Jonathan said that it could indeed be different in other places.

What luck that we had landed up here! Here in Cherry Valley, where life was as easy and simple as Jonathan had said. It couldn't be easier or simpler than on a morning like this. First you're awakened in your kitchen by the sun shining in through the window and the birds twittering and happy in the trees outside, and you see Jonathan quietly setting out bread and milk on the table for you, and when you've finished, you go out and feed your rabbits and groom your horse. And then you ride off, oh, you ride off, and there's dew on the grass, glittering and shining everywhere, and bumblebees and ordinary bees humming in the cherry blossoms, and your horse gallops away and you're not even afraid that it'll all suddenly come to an end, like everything that's fun usually does. Not in Nangiyala! At least not here in Cherry Valley!

We rode through the meadows, hither and thither as things

came, then we followed the path along the stream, twisting and turning, and suddenly we saw the morning smoke from the village down in the valley, at first just the smoke and then the whole village itself with its old houses and farms. We heard cocks crowing and dogs barking and sheep and goats bleating; it all sounded like morning, all of it. The village must have just awakened.

A woman with a basket on her arm came toward us on the path, a peasant woman, I think, neither young nor old, but a bit in between, brown-skinned as you get when you're out in all weathers. She was dressed in an old-fashioned way, rather like in the sagas.

"Oh, Jonathan, your brother's come at last, has he?" she said, smiling in a friendly way.

"Yes, he's come now," said Jonathan, and you could hear that he thought that was good. "Rusky, this is Sofia," he said then, and Sofia nodded.

"Yes, this is Sofia," she said. "I'm glad I met you. Now you can take the basket yourselves."

Jonathan took the basket as if he were used to doing that and didn't have to ask what was in it.

"You'll bring your brother down to the Golden Cockerel this evening, won't you, so that everyone can meet him?" said Sofia.

Jonathan said that he would, and then we said good-by to her and rode homeward. I asked Jonathan who the Golden Cockerel was.

"The Golden Cockerel Inn," said Jonathan. "It's the inn down in the village. We meet there and talk about what we have to talk about."

I thought it would be fun to go with him to the Golden Cockerel in the evening and see what kind of people lived in

30

Cherry Valley. I wanted to know everything about Cherry Valley and Nangiyala. I wanted to see if it was exactly like what Jonathan had told me. Then I happened to think of something, and I reminded him about it as we rode along.

"Jonathan, you said that in Nangiyala you could have adventures from morning till evening, and at night too, do you remember? But here it's so quiet and there are no adventures at all."

Jonathan laughed.

"You only came yesterday, don't forget. Silly, you've hardly had time to poke your nose in yet. There'll be time enough for adventures, I think."

When I'd got my thoughts straight on the matter, I said that it was adventurous and marvelous enough as it was with Knights Farm and our horses and rabbits and everything. I didn't need any more adventures than that.

Then Jonathan looked strangely at me, almost as if he were feeling sorry for me, and he said:

"Well, you know, Rusky, I'd like to think that that was what it would be like for you. Just like that. For I'll have you know, there are adventures that *shouldn't* happen."

When we got home, Jonathan unpacked Sofia's basket on the kitchen table. There was a loaf of bread in it and a bottle of milk, a little jar of honey, and four pancakes.

"Does Sofia keep us in food?" I asked in surprise. I hadn't thought much about how we would get anything to eat.

"Sometimes she does," said Jonathan.

"For free?" I asked.

"Free, yes, perhaps you can put it that way," said Jonathan. "Everything here in Cherry Valley is free. We give to each other and help each other according to what is needed."

"Do you give Sofia something?" I said.

Then he laughed again.

"Yes, indeed I do," he said. "Horse manure for her rose beds, among other things. I look after them for her—quite free."

And then he said so quietly that I hardly heard it:

"I do quite a lot of other things for her, too."

Just then I saw him take something else out of the basket, a tiny little rolled-up piece of paper, nothing else. He unrolled it and read something that was written on it, and then he frowned as if he didn't like what was there. But he didn't say anything to me, and I didn't like to ask. I thought he would tell me what was on his piece of paper when he wanted me to know.

We had an old sideboard in a corner of the kitchen, and on that first evening at Knights Farm, Jonathan had told me something about it. There was a secret drawer in the sideboard, he said, a drawer you could neither find nor open if you didn't know the trick. I wanted to see it at once, of course, but then Jonathan said:

"Another time. You must sleep now."

Then I fell asleep and forgot all about it, but now I remembered it again, for Jonathan went over to the sideboard and I heard a few strange little clicks. It wasn't difficult to work out what he was doing; he was hiding the piece of paper in the secret drawer. Then he locked the sideboard and put the key in an old mortar high up on a shelf in the kitchen.

Afterward we went swimming for a while and I dived off the bridge! Just think that I dared to! And then Jonathan made me a fishing rod just like his own and we caught some fish, just enough for dinner for the two of us. I got a fine perch and Jonathan got two.

We cooked the fish in our big fireplace, in a pot that hung on an iron chain over the fire, and when we had eaten, Jonathan said:

32

"Now, Rusky, we'll see if you are a marksman. You'll need to be that sometimes."

He took me out to the stable, and in the harness room two bows were hanging. I realized that Jonathan had made them, for he was always making bows for the children in the yard at home in town. But these were larger and finer, very grand objects indeed.

We set up a target on the stable door and we shot at it all afternoon. Jonathan showed me what to do. I shot quite well, though not like Jonathan, of course, because he got a bull's eye practically every time.

It was funny with Jonathan. Although he could do everything so much better than I could, he didn't think that this was anything remarkable. He never boasted, but did everything almost as if he weren't thinking about it. Sometimes I almost think he wished that I would do better than him. I got a bull's eye once, I too, and he looked so pleased then, almost as if he had gotten a present from me.

When dusk began to fall, Jonathan said it was time we were on our way to the Golden Cockerel. We whistled for Grim and Fyalar. They ran free in the meadows outside Knights Farm, but when we whistled they at once came at full gallop up to the gate. We saddled them there and mounted, and then we rode at a leisurely pace down toward the village.

Suddenly I felt afraid and shy. I was not really used to meeting people, least of all people like those who lived here in Nangiyala, and I told Jonathan.

"What are you afraid of?" he said. "You don't think there's anyone here who would harm you, do you?"

"No, of course not, but perhaps they'll laugh at me."

I thought that sounded silly when I said it, for why should they laugh at me? But I'm always imagining things like that.

"You know, I think we'll have to start calling you Karl now, now that your name's Lionheart," said Jonathan. "Rusky Lionheart—that might make them laugh. You nearly laughed your head off yourself at that, and so did I."

Yes, I wanted to be called Karl very much. It certainly suited my surname much better.

"Karl Lionheart." I tried out how it sounded. "Karl and Jonathan Lionheart are riding here." That sounded good, I thought.

"Though you're still my old Rusky," said Jonathan. "You know that, don't you, little Karl?"

We were soon down in the village and went clattering down the village street on our horses. It wasn't difficult to find our way, because we could hear laughter and talk from a long way away. And we saw the sign, too, with its large gilded cockerel; oh yes, here was the Golden Cockerel, just like those friendly old inns you used to read about in books. The lights glowed in a friendly way through the windows and you really felt like trying out what it was like to go into an inn. I'd never done that before.

But first we rode into the yard and tied Grim and Fyalar up alongside a large number of other horses standing there. That was right what Jonathan had said about your needing a horse in Nangiyala. I think every single person in Cherry Valley had come riding in to the Golden Cockerel that evening. The tap room was packed with people when we went in. Men and women, large and small, everyone in the village was there, sitting and talking and enjoying themselves, although some of the little children had already fallen asleep on their parents' laps.

What excitement there was when we came in.

"Jonathan!" they shouted. "Here's Jonathan!"

The innkeeper himself—a large, red-cheeked, rather handsome man—shouted so he could be heard above all the noise.

34

"Here's Jonathan—no, here are the two Lionheart brothers, my goodness! Both of them!"

He came forward and swung me up on a table, so that everyone could see me, and I stood there feeling my face going red all over.

But Jonathan said:

"This is my beloved brother, Karl Lionheart, who has arrived at last. You must all be kind to him, just as kind as you are to me."

"You can rely on that," said the innkeeper, and he lifted me down again. But before he let me go, he held me in his arms for a while and I felt how strong he was.

"We two," he said, "we'll be good friends like Jonathan and me. My name's Jossi. Though I'm mostly called the Golden Cockerel. And you can come to the Golden Cockerel whenever you like, don't forget that, Karl Lionheart."

Sofia was sitting there too, at a table all on her own, and Jonathan and I sat down with her. She was glad of that, I think. She smiled kindly and asked what I thought of my horse and wondered whether Jonathan could come and help her in the garden some day. But then she sat there in silence, and I noticed that she was worried about something. I noticed something else, too. Everyone sitting there in the tap room looked almost a little reverently at Sofia, and when someone got up to go, he always bowed first toward our table, just as if there were something special about her, though I couldn't understand why. She was sitting there in her simple clothes, with a shawl over her head and her brown work-roughened hands in her lap, like any ordinary peasant woman. What was it that was remarkable about her?

It was fun at the inn. We sang lots of songs, some of which I knew beforehand, and some of which I had never heard before, but everyone was happy. Or were they? Sometimes I had a feeling that they had some secret troubles, just like Sofia. It was as if they occasionally happened to think about something else, something they were afraid of. But Jonathan had said that life was easy and simple here in Cherry Valley, so what were they afraid of? Oh, well, between times, they were happy, they sang and laughed and everyone was good friends and liked each other, it seemed. But I think they liked Jonathan best. It was just like at home in town; everyone liked him. And Sofia, they liked her, too, I think.

Though afterward, when we were going home, Jonathan and I, and we were going out into the yard to get our horses, I asked:

"Jonathan, what is it that's so special about Sofia?"

Then we heard a grumpy voice beside us say:

"Exactly! What is there so special about Sofia, I've often wondered."

It was dark in the yard, so I couldn't see who was speaking. But suddenly, he stepped forward into the light from the window, and I recognized a man who had sat near us in the inn, a man with red, curly hair and a little red beard. I had noticed him because he had sat looking surly all the time and hadn't sung at all.

"Who's that?" I asked Jonathan, as we clattered out through the entrance.

"His name is Hubert," said Jonathan. "And he knows perfectly well what's special about Sofia."

Then we rode homeward. It was a chilly, starlit night. Never have I seen so many stars and never such brilliant ones. I tried to guess which was the Earth Star.

But Jonathan said: "The Earth Star, well, that wanders about somewhere far, far away in space; you can't see it from here."

That was a little sad, I thought.

CHAPTER FIVE

BUT THEN THE DAY CAME WHEN I FOUND OUT what was special about Sofia.

One morning, Jonathan said:

"We're going over to the Queen of the Pigeons for a while today."

"That sounds grand," I said. "What kind of queen is that?"

"Sofia," said Jonathan. "The Queen of the Pigeons—I call her that for fun."

I soon knew why.

It was quite a way to Tulip Farm, where Sofia lived. Her house was on the outskirts of Cherry Valley, with the high mountains just behind it.

We rode over there in the morning, and Sofia was standing there feeding her pigeons, all her snow-white pigeons. When I saw them, I remembered her, that white one that sat on my windowsill, at least a thousand years ago now.

"Do you remember?" I whispered to Jonathan. "Wasn't it

one of those pigeons that lent you the protection of its feathers when—when you came to me?"

"Yes," said Jonathan. "How could I have gone otherwise? Sofia's pigeons are the only ones that can fly through the skies as far as they like."

The pigeons were like a white cloud around Sofia, and she was standing there quite still in the middle, surrounded by the flapping of their wings. It was exactly what a Queen of the Pigeons should look like, I thought.

Then she caught sight of us. She greeted us kindly, as usual, but she wasn't happy. She was quite sorrowful and at once said in a low voice to Jonathan:

"I found Violanta dead with an arrow in her breast last night. Up in Wolf Gorge. And the message had gone."

Jonathan's eyes darkened. I had never seen him like that, never seen him so embittered. I recognized neither him nor his voice.

"That means it's as I thought," he said. "We've got a traitor in Cherry Valley."

"Yes, I think we have," said Sofia. "I didn't want to believe it. But now I see that it must be true."

You could see how sad she was, and yet she turned to me and said:

"Come, Karl, you must come and look around my place all the same."

She lived alone at Tulip Farm with her pigeons and her bees and her goats, with a garden so full of flowers that you could hardly make your way through it.

While Sofia took me around, Jonathan started digging and weeding in that way you have to in the spring.

I looked at everything, Sofia's many beehives and her tulips and narcissuses and her inquisitive goats, but all the time I kept

thinking about that Violanta, whoever that was, who had been shot up there in the mountains.

We soon went back to Jonathan, who was on his knees weeding so hard that his fingers were black.

Sofia looked sorrowfully at him and then said:

"Listen, my little gardener's boy, I think that you'll soon have to get to work on something else now."

"I can see that," said Jonathan.

Poor Sofia, she was more worried than she wished us to see, I suppose. She went and gazed up toward the mountains, looking so troubled that I grew anxious too. What was she looking for? Who was she expecting?

We were soon to know, because suddenly Sofia said:

"There she is! Thank God, there's Paloma!"

It was one of her pigeons that came flying in; at first it was nothing but a little speck against the mountains, but soon she was with us, landing on Sofia's shoulder.

"Come, Jonathan," said Sofia quickly.

"Yes, but Rusky—I mean Karl," said Jonathan. "He must be told all about it now, mustn't he?"

"Of course," said Sofia. "Hurry now, both of you."

With the pigeon on her shoulder, Sofia ran ahead of us into the house. She took us into a little room off the kitchen, and then she bolted the door and closed the shutters. I suppose she wanted to be sure that no one could either see or hear what we were doing.

"Paloma, my pigeon," said Sofia. "Have you a better message than the last one with you today?"

She thrust her hand under one of the pigeon's wings and brought out a little capsule. Out of it, she took a tiny roll of paper, just like the one I had seen Jonathan take out of the basket and hide in the sideboard at home.

40

"Read it quickly," said Jonathan. "Quickly, quickly!"

Sofia read it and let out a little cry.

"They've taken Orvar, too," she said. "Now there's no one left there who can really do anything."

She handed the piece of paper to Jonathan, and as he read it, his eyes darkened even more.

"A traitor in Cherry Valley," he said. "Who do you think it is that can be such a wretch?"

"I don't know," said Sofia. "Not yet. But God help him, whoever he is, when I find out."

I was sitting there listening and not understanding a thing.

Sofia sighed and then said:

"You must tell Karl. I'll go and get some breakfast for you in the meantime."

She vanished into the kitchen.

Jonathan sat down on the floor with his back against the wall. He sat there in silence, looking at his muddy fingers, but finally he said:

"Well, I'll tell you now. Now that Sofia has said that I may."

He had told me a great deal about Nangiyala, both before I had come and afterward, but nothing like what I was told there in Sofia's room.

"You remember that I said," he began, "that life here in Cherry Valley was easy and simple. It has been like that, and it should be like that, but it is not likely to be like that any longer. For when it's miserable and difficult over there in the other valley, then life becomes difficult in Cherry Valley too, you see."

"Is there more than one valley?" I asked, and then Jonathan told me about Nangiyala's two green valleys that lay there so beautifully in among Nangiyala's mountains—Cherry Valley and Wild Rose Valley, deep valleys with mountains around them, high, wild mountains that were difficult to cross if you did not know the twisting dangerous little paths, Jonathan said. But the people in the valleys knew the paths and could travel freely to see each other.

"Or to put it more accurately, they used to be able to," said Jonathan. "Now no one is allowed out of Wild Rose Valley and no one can get in there, either. Only Sofia's pigeons."

"Why not?" I said.

"Because Wild Rose Valley is no longer a free country," said Jonathan. "Because that valley is in enemy hands."

He looked at me as if he were sorry to have to frighten me.

"And no one knows what will happen to Cherry Valley," he said.

I was afraid then. I had been going around so calmly, thinking that there was nothing dangerous in Nangiyala, but now I was truly frightened.

"What sort of enemy is it?" I asked.

"His name's Tengil," said Jonathan, and he spoke the name so that it sounded horrible and dangerous.

"Where is Tengil?" I said.

Then Jonathan told me about Karmanyaka, the country up in the mountains of The Ancient Mountains, beyond the river of The Ancient Rivers, where Tengil ruled, cruel as a serpent.

I grew even more afraid but I didn't want to show it.

"Why can't he stay there in his ancient mountains?" I said. "Why does he have to come to Nangiyala and destroy things?"

"Well, you know," said Jonathan. "The person who can answer that one can answer a great deal. I don't know why he has to spoil everything there is. It's just like that. He begrudges the people in the valleys the life they lead. And he needs bondsmen."

Then he sat silent again, staring at his hands, but he did mumble something and I heard it.

"The monster has Katla too!"

Katla! I don't know why that sounded more horrible than everything else that he had said, and I asked him:

"Who's Katla?"

But Jonathan shook his head.

"No, Rusky, I know that you are already scared. I don't want to talk about Katla, because then you won't sleep tonight."

Instead he told me what it was that was so special about Sofia.

"She is the leader of our secret struggle against Tengil," said Jonathan. "We fight against him, you see, to help Wild Rose Valley. Though we have to do it secretly."

"But Sofia," I said. "Why just her?"

"Because she's strong and knows about things like that," said Jonathan. "And because she's not the slightest bit afraid."

"Afraid? But you're not afraid, either, Jonathan, are you?"

He thought for a while and then he said:

"No, I'm not afraid, either."

Oh, how I wished that I could be as brave as Sofia and Jonathan. But instead I was sitting there so terrified that I could hardly think.

"This business with Sofia and her pigeons flying with secret messages over the mountains, is that something that *everyone* knows about?"

"Only the people whom we can definitely trust," said Jonathan. "But among them there's *one* traitor, and that's enough."

Now his eyes darkened again and he said sorrowfully:

"Violanta had a secret message with her from Sofia when she was shot down last night. And if that message has fallen into Tengil's hands, that means death for many people over in Wild Rose Valley."

I thought it was horrible that anyone could shoot a pigeon

which came flying by, so white and innocent, even if she did have a secret message on her.

And suddenly I remembered what we had in the sideboard at home. I asked Jonathan why we should have secret messages in our sideboard. Wouldn't that be dangerous?

"Yes, it's dangerous," said Jonathan. "Though it'd be even more dangerous to keep them at Sofia's. Tengil's spies would search there first of all if they came to Cherry Valley, and not the house of her gardener's boy."

That was what was so good, Jonathan said. No one except Sofia knew who he really was, that he wasn't just her gardener's boy but also her closest man in the struggle against Tengil.

"Sofia decided that herself," he said. "She didn't want a single person here in Cherry Valley to know, and so you must swear to keep quiet until the day Sofia tells everyone about it."

And I swore that I'd rather die than betray anything I had heard.

We had breakfast at Sofia's and then we rode home.

There was someone else out riding that morning, someone we met on the path just as we were leaving Tulip Farm. The man with the red beard—what was his name, now? Hubert?

"Oh, so you've been to see Sofia," said Hubert. "What have you been doing there?"

"Weeding her garden," said Jonathan, holding up his muddy fingers. "And you, are you out hunting?" he said, for Hubert had his bow in front of him on the pommel of his saddle.

"Yes, I'm going to get myself a couple of rabbits," said Hubert.

I thought of our small rabbits at home, and I was glad when Hubert trotted his horse away, so that I no longer had to see him.

"Hubert," I said to Jonathan. "What do you think of him?"

Jonathan thought for a while.

"He's the best marksman in the whole of Cherry Valley."

He didn't say anything else but urged on his horse and we rode on.

Jonathan had taken Paloma's message with him, pushed into a little leather bag under his shirt, and when we got home he put the piece of paper into the secret drawer in the sideboard. But first I was allowed to read what was on it, and this is what it said: "*Orvar was caught yesterday and is now imprisoned in Katla Cavern. Someone in Cherry Valley must have betrayed his hiding place. You have a traitor there. Find out who.*"

"Find out who," said Jonathan. "I wish I could."

There was more in the message but it was written in some secret language that I didn't understand, and Jonathan said I needn't know it. It was just something Sofia had to know about.

But he showed me how to open the secret drawer. I was allowed to open it and close it several times. Then he closed it himself and locked the sideboard and put the key back in the mortar.

All that day I thought about what I'd been told, and that night I didn't sleep very well. I dreamt about Tengil and dead pigeons and the prisoner in Katla Cavern and I cried out in my sleep, so that it woke me up.

And then—believe it or not—then I saw someone standing in the dark corner over by the sideboard, someone who was frightened when I cried out and vanished like a dark shadow through the door, before I'd even woken up properly.

It all happened so quickly that I almost thought I'd dreamt it all, but Jonathan didn't think so when I woke him and told him.

"Oh, no, Rusky, that was no dream," he said. "That was certainly no dream but the traitor!"

CHAPTER SIX

"TENGIL'S TIME WILL COME ONE DAY," Jonathan said. We were lying in the green grass down by the stream, and it was one of those mornings when you simply cannot believe that Tengil or any other evil in the world exists. It was perfectly still and peaceful, the water bubbling slightly around the stones under the bridge the only sound you could hear. It was lovely, lying there on your back, seeing nothing at all either, except the little white clouds up in the sky. You could lie like that and feel happy and sing a little to yourself, not bothering about anything.

And then Jonathan started talking about Tengil! I didn't want to remember him, but all the same I said:

"What do you mean by that? That Tengil's time will come?"

"That what'll happen to him happens to all tyrants sooner or later," said Jonathan. "That he'll be crushed like a louse and will be gone forever."

"I hope it'll happen soon," I said.

There was a little mumble from Jonathan.

46

"Though he's strong, Tengil. And he's got Katla!"

Again he had said that terrible name. I wanted to ask him about it but I didn't. It was just as well not to know anything about Katla on such a lovely morning.

But then Jonathan said something even worse than everything else.

"Rusky, you're going to be alone at Knights Farm for a while. For I've got to go to Wild Rose Valley."

How *could* he say anything so terrible? How could he think that I would stay at Knights Farm for a single minute without him? If he was thinking of hurling himself straight into Tengil's jaws, then I was going to be with him and I told him so.

Then he looked at me very strangely and said:

"Rusky, I have only one brother, whom I wish to protect from all evil. How can you ask me to take you with me when I need all my strength for something else? Something that's really dangerous."

That didn't help at all. I was sad and angry so that everything boiled inside me, and I cried out:

"And you, how can you ask that I stay alone at Knights Farm, waiting for you, when perhaps you'll never come back?"

I remembered suddenly how things had been that time when Jonathan was dead and away from me, and I was lying in my sofa-bed, not knowing whether I'd ever see him again; oh, it was like looking down into a black hole, just thinking about it.

And now he wanted to leave me again, just disappear into dangers about which I knew nothing, and if he didn't come back, this time there would be no help and I'd be alone forever and ever.

I could feel myself getting angrier and angrier, and I shouted at him even louder and said as many horrible things as I could think up.

It was not easy for him to calm me down, even a little. But, of course, things went as he wished in the end. I knew that he understood everything better than I did.

"Silly, of course I'm coming back," he said. That was in the evening as we were sitting warming ourselves by the fire in our kitchen, the evening before he was to leave.

I wasn't angry any longer, only sad, and Jonathan knew it. He was kind to me. He gave me newly baked bread with butter and honey on it, and told me sagas and stories, but I couldn't listen to them. I thought about the saga of Tengil, which I was beginning to think was the cruelest of all sagas. I asked Jonathan why he had to undertake something so dangerous. Couldn't he just as well stay at home by the fire at Knights Farm and enjoy himself? But then Jonathan said there were things you have to do even if they are dangerous.

"Why?" I said.

"Otherwise you aren't a human being but just a bit of filth."

He had told me what he was going to do. He was going to rescue Orvar from Katla Cavern. For Orvar was even more important than Sofia, Jonathan said, and without Orvar it was probably the end of Nangiyala's green valleys.

It was late now, the fire out on the hearth, and night had come.

Then the day came, and I stood at the gate and watched Jonathan ride away, disappearing into the mist; there was mist all over Cherry Valley that morning. And you must believe me when I say it was as if my heart would break, when he just become blurred and vanished. And I was left alone. It was unbearable. I was as if mad with grief and I ran to the stable and got Fyalar out and threw myself into the saddle and set off after Jonathan. I had to see him once more, before I lost him forever.

He was going to Tulip Farm first, to get his orders from Sofia,

I knew that, and so I rode there. I rode like a maniac and I caught up with him just outside the farm. Then I was almost ashamed and wanted to hide, but he'd already heard and seen me.

"What do you want?" he said.

Well, what did I want?

"Are you sure you're coming back?" I mumbled. It was all I could think of saying.

Then he rode up beside me and our horses stood side by side. Jonathan wiped something off my cheek, tears or something, with his forefinger, and said:

"Don't cry, Rusky. We'll meet again—I promise you. And if it's not here, it'll be in Nangilima."

"Nangilima?" I said. "What's that now?"

"I'll tell you another time," said Jonathan.

I don't understand how I withstood being alone at Knights Farm, or how I got the days to go by. I looked after my animals, of course. I was in the stable with Fyalar most of the time, and for long spells I talked to my rabbits. I fished a little and practiced shooting with my bow and arrows, but everything seemed so pointless when Jonathan wasn't there. Sofia brought food for me now and then, and we talked about Jonathan. I kept hoping she would say, "he'll be coming home shortly," but she didn't. I also wanted to ask her why she didn't go herself to try to save Orvar instead of sending Jonathan. But why should I ask, when I knew the answer.

Tengil hated Sofia, Jonathan had explained to me.

"Sofia in Cherry Valley and Orvar in Wild Rose Valley, they're his worst enemies, and you can be sure he knows it," Jonathan had said when he was telling me how things were.

"He's got Orvar in Katla Cavern and he'd like to put Sofia in there too, to pine away and die. The wretch, he's promised fif-teen white horses as a reward to the person who hands over Sofia dead or alive to him."

Jonathan told me that. So of course I understood why Sofia had to keep away from Wild Rose Valley and why Jonathan had to go instead. Tengil knew nothing about him, they thought, or so they hoped. Though there was someone who had realized that Jonathan was not just a gardener's boy: the person who had come to our place in the night, the person I'd seen over by the sideboard. Sofia couldn't help worrying about him.

"That man knows too much," she said.

She asked me to send a message over to her if anyone else came snooping around Knights Farm. I said that it was no use anyone trying the sideboard again, because we had moved all the secret papers to another place. Now we had them in the oat bin in the harness room, in a large snuff box which was hidden under all the oats.

Sofia went with me to the harness room and dug up the snuff box and put another message into it. It was a good hiding place, she thought, and I thought so too.

"Stick it out if you can," said Sofia as she was leaving. "I know it's difficult but you must stick with it."

It was difficult, too, especially in the evenings and at night. I dreamt terrible dreams about Jonathan and worried about him every waking moment, too.

One evening I rode down to the Golden Cockerel. I couldn't bear just sitting at home at Knights Farm, it was so quiet and my thoughts could be heard only too well; they weren't the kind of thoughts that cheered you up.

They all stared at me; yes, they did, when I came into the inn without Jonathan.

"What now?" said Jossi. "Only half of the Lionheart brothers! What have you done with Jonathan?"

It was difficult for me. I remembered what Sofia and Jonathan had preached to me. Whatever happened, I must not tell anyone what Jonathan was doing and where he had gone. Not a single living person! So I pretended I hadn't heard Jossi's question. But Hubert was sitting there at his table, and he wanted to know too.

"Yes, where's Jonathan?" he said. "Surely Sofia hasn't got rid of her gardener's boy?"

"Jonathan's out hunting," I said. "He's up in the mountains hunting wolves."

I had to say something and I thought that was a good invention, for Jonathan had said there were a lot of wolves here and there in the mountains.

Sofia wasn't at the inn that evening, but otherwise the whole village was there, as usual. And they sang their songs and enjoyed themselves, as usual. But I didn't sing with them because, for me, things weren't as usual. Without Jonathan, I didn't like it there, so I didn't stay long.

"Don't look so sad, Karl Lionheart," said Jossi as I was leaving. "Jonathan will soon have finished hunting, and then he'll be home."

Oh, how I liked him for saying that! He patted my cheek, too, and gave me a few delicious cakes to take home with me.

"You can put those inside you when you're sitting there at home, waiting for Jonathan," he said.

He was kind, the Golden Cockerel. It seemed almost slightly less lonely just because of that.

I rode home with my cakes and sat in front of the fire eating them. It was warm spring weather now in the daytime, almost summer, and yet I still had to light our big fire, for the warmth of the sun had not yet managed to get through the thick walls of our house.

It felt cold as I crept into my cupboard-bed, but I soon fell asleep. And I dreamt about Jonathan, a dream so terrifying that it woke me up.

"Yes, Jonathan!" I cried. "I'm coming!" I cried, and I rushed out of bed. In the darkness around me, there seemed to be echoes of wild cries, Jonathan's cries! He had called to me in my dream that he needed help. I knew it. I could still hear him, and I wanted to rush straight out into the dark night to get to him, wherever he was. But I realized how impossible that was. What could I do? No one was so helpless as I was! I could only creep back into my bed again and lie there trembling, feeling lost and small and afraid and lonely, the loneliest person in the whole world, I thought.

Neither did it help all that much when morning came and it was a bright, clear day. Of course, it was harder then to remember exactly how terrible the dream had been, but that Jonathan had cried out for help I couldn't forget. My brother had called for me, so didn't I have to go out and try to find him?

I sat for hours out with my rabbits and thought about what I should do. I had no one to talk to, no one to ask. I had to decide for myself. I couldn't go to Sofia because she would stop me. She would never let me go; she was not that foolish. For it was foolish, I'm sure, what I wanted to do. And dangerous too. The most dangerous thing of all. And I wasn't at all brave.

I don't know how long I sat there, leaning against the stable wall, tearing up grass. I tore off every blade of grass round about me, but I didn't notice until afterward, not while I'd been sitting there being tormented. The hours went by; perhaps I would be sitting there still, if I hadn't suddenly remembered what Jonathan had said—that sometimes you have to do things that are dangerous; otherwise you weren't a human being but a bit of filth.

So I decided. I banged my fist down on the rabbit hutch so

that the rabbits jumped, and I said out loud so there would be no mistake.

"I'll do it! I'll do it! I'm not a bit of filth."

Oh, how good it felt to have decided!

"I know I'm right," I said to the rabbits, for I had no one else to talk to.

The rabbits—well, they'd have to become wild rabbits now. I took them out of the hutch and carried them in my arms to the gate and showed them the lovely green Cherry Valley.

"The whole valley is full of grass," I said, "and there are lots of other rabbits you can be with there. I think you'll have much more fun than in a hutch, but just watch out for the fox and Hubert."

The three of them seemed a little surprised and scampered about a bit as if they were wondering whether this could possibly be right. But then they made off and vanished in a flash in among the green hummocks.

Then I hurried to get things ready, gathering together everything I was to take with me. A blanket to wrap around me when I had to sleep. A tinderbox to make a fire with. A nosebag full of oats for Fyalar. And a sack of food for myself. Well, I had nothing but bread, but that was the best bread, Sofia's ring loaves. She'd come over with a whole pile of them, and I stuffed the sack full. That'll last a long time, I thought, and when it's all gone, I'll have to eat grass like the rabbits.

Sofia was going to bring some soup the next day, she had promised, but by then I would already be far away. Poor Sofia, she would have to eat her own soup, but I couldn't let her just wonder where I'd gone. She would have to know, though not until it was too late. Too late to stop me.

I took a bit of charcoal from the hearth and wrote in large letters on the kitchen wall: "Someone called me in my dream, and I've gone to find him far, far away beyond the mountains."

I wrote it in that funny way, because I thought that if some-one besides Sofia came to Knights Farm, someone snooping, then he wouldn't know what it meant. He would perhaps think I had tried to write a poem or something. But Sofia would at once understand what I meant; I'm away looking for Jonathan.

I was glad and for once felt really strong and brave. I sang to myself.

"Someone called to me in my dream, and I've gone to find him far, far away beyond the mounta-a-a-a-ains," and oh, how good it sounded. I would have to tell Jonathan all this when I found him, I thought.

If I find him, I thought then. But if I didn't . . .

Then my courage ran out of me all at once. I was a little bit of filth again, a scared little bit of filth, as I'd always been. And then I longed for Fyalar as usual. I had to go out to him im-mediately. That was the only thing that helped a little when I was sad and anxious. How many times had I stood with him in his stall, when I couldn't bear to be alone? How many times hadn't it comforted me just to look at his wise eyes and feel that he was warm and his nose was soft? Without Fyalar, I couldn't have lived through that time when Jonathan was away.

I ran to the stable.

Fyalar was not alone in his stall. Hubert was standing there. Yes, Hubert was standing there, patting my horse and grinning when he caught sight of me.

My heart began to thump.

He's the traitor, I thought. I think I'd felt this for a long time, and now I was certain. Hubert was the traitor. Otherwise why did he come snooping around Knights Farm?

"That man knows too much," Sofia had said, and Hubert was that man. I realized that now.

How much did he know? Did he know everything? Did he know what we'd hidden in the oat bin too? I tried not to show how frightened I was.

"What are you doing here?" I said as assertively as I could. "What do you want with Fyalar?"

"Nothing," said Hubert. "I was on my way to you, but I heard your horse whinny and I like horses. He's fine, Fyalar."

You can't trip me up, I thought, and I said:

"What do you want of me, then?"

"To give you this," said Hubert, and he handed me something wrapped up in a white cloth. "You looked so sad and hungry last night that I thought perhaps you were short of food here on Knights Farm, with Jonathan away hunting."

Now I didn't know what to say or do. I muttered my thanks. But I couldn't take food from a traitor! Or could I?

I fumbled with the piece of cloth and found a large piece of mutton, dried, smoked mutton which is so good, spring fiddle, it's called, I think.

It smelled wonderful. I felt like sinking my teeth into it at once, though I should really have told Hubert to take his spring fiddle away and himself with it.

But I didn't. It was Sofia's task to deal with traitors. I would have to pretend that I knew nothing and understood nothing. Actually, I very much wanted the meat because nothing could be better than that for my food sack.

Hubert was still standing by Fyalar.

"You really have got a fine horse," he said. "Almost as fine as my Blenda."

"Blenda is white," I said. "Do you like white horses?"

"Yes, I like white horses very much," said Hubert.

Then you'd like to have fifteen, wouldn't you? I thought, but I didn't say it. Instead Hubert said something terrible:

"Shouldn't we give Fyalar a few oats? He should have something nice, too."

I couldn't stop him. He went straight into the harness room and I ran after him. I wanted to shout "Stop it," but couldn't get a word out.

Hubert opened the lid of the oat bin and picked up the scoop that was lying on top. I closed my eyes because I didn't want to see him scoop up the snuff box. But then I heard him swear, and when I opened my eyes I saw a little rat come diving over the edge of the bin. Hubert tried to kick her, but she ran away across the stable floor and disappeared into some secret hole.

"She bit my thumb, the wretch," said Hubert. He was standing there inspecting his thumb, and then I took my chance. Quickly, quickly, I filled the scoop with oats and then I slammed down the bin lid right in front of Hubert's nose.

"Fyalar will be pleased," I said. "He's not used to getting oats at this time of day."

But you're not quite so pleased, I thought, as Hubert curtly said good-by and slouched off through the stable door.

He didn't get his paws on any secret messages that time, but now it was necessary to find a new hiding place. I thought for a long time and in the end buried the snuff box in the potato cellar, inside the door on the left.

And then I wrote on the kitchen wall a new puzzle for Sofia. "Red beard wants white horses and knows too much. Watch out!"

I couldn't do more for Sofia.

At sunrise the next morning, before anyone in Cherry Valley was awake, I left Knights Farm and rode up toward the mountains.

CHAPTER SEVEN

I TOLD FYALAR WHAT IT FELT LIKE TO BE ME, just me, out on a long ride in the mountains.

"Do you realize what an adventure this is for me? Remember that I've done nothing but lie on a sofa-bed nearly all my life! You mustn't think that I forget Jonathan for one single minute. But otherwise I'd shout so that it rang around the mountains, just because this is so wonderful."

It *was* wonderful. Jonathan would understand that. What mountains; just imagine that such high ones existed, that so many clear little lakes and rushing streams and waterfalls and meadows full of spring flowers existed, right up in the mountains. And there was I, Rusky, on my horse, seeing it all! I didn't know that anything in the world could be so beautiful, so at first I was quite dizzy.

But gradually it changed. I had found a little bridle path, probably the one Jonathan had told me about. Through twists and turns, that's how you get to Wild Rose Valley, he had said. Twists and turns there certainly were. Soon I had twisted and turned my way away from the meadows, and the mountains became wilder and more and more terrible and the path more and more dangerous to move along. Sometimes it climbed steeply, sometimes it plunged down, sometimes it wound its way along narrow rock shelves alongside huge precipices, and then I thought I would never manage. But Fyalar must have been very used to making his way along dangerous mountain paths. He was fine, Fyalar.

Toward evening, we were tired, both I and my horse, so then I made camp for the night on a little green patch where Fyalar could graze, close to a stream where we both could drink.

Then I made a campfire. All my life I had longed to be able to sit by a campfire, for Jonathan had told me how wonderful it was; and now at last I was.

"Now, Rusky, at last you'll know what it feels like," I said out loud to myself.

I collected some dry branches and twigs into a large heap and lit a bonfire, which burned and crackled, so that the sparks flew, and I sat by my fire and felt that it was exactly as Jonathan had said. I felt wonderful as I sat there, looking into the flames, eating my bread and chewing on my smoked meat, which was so delicious I only wished I'd been given it by someone other than Hubert.

I was happy and I sang to myself a little in my solitude. "My bread and my fire and my horse! My bread and my fire and my horse!"—I couldn't think of anything else.

I sat like that for a long time and I thought of all the campfires that had burned in all the wildernesses of the world since the beginning of time, and how they had all gone out long ago. But mine was burning here and now!

It grew dark around me. The mountains grew black—oh, how

dark it was and how quickly it happened. I didn't like having my back to all that darkness. It felt as if someone might come at me from behind. Anyhow, it was time to sleep now, so I stoked up the fire well and said goodnight to Fyalar and rolled myself up in my blanket as close to the fire as I could. Then I wished I could just fall asleep at once before I could frighten myself.

Yes, I could frighten myself, only too quickly. I don't know anyone who can do that as quickly as I can. My thoughts began to grind around in my head—there was sure to be someone lurking out there in the darkness, and Tengil's soldiers and spies were sure to be seething all over the mountains here, and Jonathan was sure to be dead long ago; that was how my thoughts went, and I didn't sleep.

Just then the moon rose behind a mountain peak; it probably wasn't the same old moon, I suppose, but it looked just the same, and I had never seen such moonlight before. But then I'd never seen moonlight over high mountains.

Everything became so strange; you were in a mysterious world of nothing but silver and black shadows. It was beautiful and a little melancholy in a lovely, strange way, but creepy, too, for although it was light where the moon shone, among the shadows any number of dangers might be hiding.

I pulled the blanket over my head because I didn't want to look any more. But then I *heard* instead, yes, I heard something: a howl far away in the mountains, and then several howls a little closer. Fyalar whinnied; he was afraid, and then I realized what it was. Wolves howling.

Someone as timid as I am could easily have died of fright, but when I noticed how anxious Fyalar was, I tried to put on a brave face.

"Fyalar, wolves are afraid of fire, didn't you know?" I said.

But I didn't really believe it, and the wolves had never heard it, either. For now I could see them; they were coming closer, horrible gray shapes which came streaking out into the moonlight, howling with hunger.

Then I howled, too. I shouted to high heaven. Never have I let out such a shout, and that frightened them a little, I think.

But not for long. Soon they were back again, even closer this time. Their howls made Fyalar quite wild. And me too. I knew we were going to die now, both of us. I should have been used to that since I'd already died once. But then I had *wanted* to, then I had longed to, and now I didn't want to. Now I wanted to live and be with Jonathan; oh, Jonathan, if only you could come and help me.

The wolves were close now. One was larger than the others and more insolent, probably the leader. He was the one who would get me, I knew. He circled around me and howled, howled so that my blood froze. I threw a burning branch at him and shouted loudly, but that just annoyed him. I saw his open jaws and his terrible teeth that were straining to get at my throat. Now—Jonathan, help! Now he's leaping!

But then! What in the world happened then? In the middle of his leap, he gave a yelp and fell down at my feet. Dead, stone dead, and straight through his head was an arrow.

From what bow did the arrow come? Who was it who had saved my life? Someone stepped out of the shadows behind a rock. Who but Hubert! There he was, looking slightly contemptuous as usual, and yet I still wanted to rush up to him and put my arms around him, I was so glad to see him. At first. But only at first.

"I seem to have come just in time," he said.

"Yes, you certainly did," I said.

"Why aren't you at home at Knights Farm?" he said.

What about you? I thought—for now I remembered who he was. What cunning treachery was to happen here in the mountains tonight? Oh, why should it be a traitor who had saved me? Why must I be grateful to Hubert, of all people, not just for the meat, but also for dear life?

"What are you doing by yourself up here in the middle of the night?" I said surlily.

"Shooting wolves, as you see," said Hubert. "Actually, I saw you when you rode away this morning, and I thought perhaps I'd see that nothing dangerous happened to you. So I followed you."

Yes, lie away, I thought. Sooner or later you'll have Sofia to deal with, and then I'll be sorry for you.

"Where is Jonathan?" said Hubert. "He, who's supposed to be out hunting wolves, should have been here to shoot a few."

I looked around. The wolves had disappeared, every one of them. They had probably been frightened when their leader had fallen dead, and perhaps they were grieving, too, for I heard plaintive little howls far away in the mountains.

"Well, where's Jonathan?" persisted Hubert, and then I had to lie, too.

"He's coming soon," I said. "He went after a wolfpack over there," I said, pointing up the mountain.

Hubert grinned. He didn't believe me, I could see that.

"Shouldn't you perhaps come with me back home to Cherry Valley, all the same?" he said.

"No, I must wait for Jonathan," I said. "He'll be here any minute now."

"Oh, yes," said Hubert. "Oh, yes," he said, looking strangely at me. And then—then he drew out the knife he had in his belt, and I let out a little cry. What was he going to do? As he stood there in the moonlight with the knife in his hand, he frightened me more than all the wolves in the mountains put together.

He wants me dead, went through my head. He knows that I know that he's the traitor, so he's followed me and now he wants to kill me.

I began to shake, my whole body began to shake.

"Don't do it," I cried. "Don't do it!"

"Don't do what?" said Hubert.

"Don't kill me," I cried.

Then Hubert turned white with rage and rushed at me, coming so close that I almost fell backward, I was so scared.

"You little scamp, what are you saying?"

He grabbed me by the hair and shook me.

"You silly dolt," he said. "If I'd wanted to see you dead, I could have left that to the wolf."

He held the knife right under my nose, and it was a sharp knife, I could see that.

"I use this to skin wolves," he said. "Not to kill stupid kids."

I got such a kick in the backside that I fell on my face, and then he set about skinning the wolf, swearing all the time as he did so.

I hurried to mount Fyalar, for I wanted to get away from that place; oh, how I wanted to get away.

"Where are you off to?" shouted Hubert.

"I think I'll go and meet Jonathan," I said, and I could hear how scared and feeble I sounded.

"Yes, do that, you oaf," shouted Hubert. "Just go and kill yourself, I won't stop you any longer."

But by then I was already riding away at full speed and could ignore Hubert.

In front of me in the moonlight the path wound its way farther up the mountain. Gentle moonlight it was, almost like daylight, so that you could see everything. What luck! Otherwise I would have been lost. It was like riding in a dream, for there were precipices and chasms which made you dizzy; how terrible and how beautiful it was! It was like riding in a dream: yes, that moonlight landscape could only exist in some lovely wild dream, I thought, and I said to Fyalar:

"Who do you think is dreaming it? Not me. There must be someone else who has been able to dream up something so unnaturally terrible and beautiful; perhaps it was God?"

But I was so tired and sleepy that I could hardly stay in the saddle. I would have to rest somewhere for the night.

"Preferably where there aren't any wolves," I said to Fyalar, and I think he agreed with that.

Who, then, had tramped up the mountain paths between Nangiyala's valleys from the beginning? Who had thought out how this path to Wild Rose Valley should go? Was it necessary to let it curve its way along such miserable little rocky outcrops, beside such terrible precipices? I knew that if Fyalar as much as put one foot down wrong, then we'd hurtle down into the depths, both of us, and then no one in an eternity of eternities would know what had happened to Karl Lionheart and his horse.

It got worse and worse; in the end, I didn't dare keep my eyes open, for if we were going to plunge down into the abyss, then I didn't want to see it.

But Fyalar didn't put a foot down wrong. He managed, and when I eventually dared to look up again, we had come to a little glade, a fine green glade which had the high, high mountains on one side and a steep precipice on the other.

"This is the place, Fyalar," I said. "Here we're safe from the wolves."

It was true. No wolf could come climbing down from the mountains since they were too high, and no wolf could come climbing out of the depths, for the cliffs were too steep. If he

were to come, the wolf, then he would have to make his way like us along the precipices on that wretched path. But they were probably not that cunning, I decided.

Then I saw something really good. There was a deep cleft right in the mountainside. A cave, you could almost call it, for there were great blocks of rock like a roof. In that cave we could sleep safely, with a roof over our heads as well.

Someone had rested in this glade before me, for there were ashes left from a campfire. I almost felt like lighting one, but I didn't have the energy. Now I only wanted to sleep. So I took Fyalar by the reins and led him into the cave. It was a deep cave, and I said to Fyalar:

"There's room for fifteen like you here."

He whinnied a little. Perhaps he was homesick for his stable. I asked his forgiveness for dragging him into this kind of hardship, and I gave him some oats and said goodnight to him again. Then I rolled myself up in my blanket in the darkest, darkest corner of the cave and fell asleep like a log, before I had time to scare myself one little bit.

I don't know how long I had been asleep, but suddenly I sat up and was wide-awake. I heard voices, and I heard horses whinnying outside my cave.

It was enough. The great wild terror swept over me again. Who knows, perhaps those people talking out there were worse than any wolves?

"Drive the horses into the cave, then we'll have more room," I heard a voice say, and then two horses clattered inside. They whinnied when they noticed Fyalar, and Fyalar whinnied back, but then they were quiet and they must have become friends in the darkness. The people outside couldn't have realized that it was a strange horse they had heard, for they calmly went on talking to each other.

66

Why had they come? Who were they? What were they doing up in the mountains at night? I would have to find out. I was so scared that my teeth chattered and I wished myself a thousand miles away. But I was there, and quite near me were some people who *might* be friends, but who might just as well be enemies, and I would have to find out which, however terrified I was. So I lay down flat on my stomach and began to crawl toward the voices out there. The moon was right in the cave entrance and a ray of moonlight fell straight down onto my hiding place, but I kept in the dark at the side, and wriggled slowly, slowly, nearer to the voices.

They were sitting out in the moonlight and were building a fire, two men with coarse faces and black helmets on their heads. It was the first time I'd seen any of Tengil's soldiers, and I knew what it was I was looking at. I knew that here were two of those cruel men who had joined Tengil to destroy the green valleys of Nangiyala. I didn't want to fall into their hands; I'd rather the wolf took me.

They were talking quietly to each other, but inside in the darkness I was so close to them that I could hear every word. They seemed to be angry with someone, for one of them said:

"I'll hack his ears off, if he doesn't come in time this time either."

And then the other man said:

"Yes, he's got a lot to learn. We have to sit here waiting in vain, night after night. What use is he, anyhow? Shooting carrier pigeons, that's all right, but Tengil wants more than that. He wants Sofia in Katla Cavern, and if this man can't fix that, it'll be the worse for him."

Then I realized that the man they were talking about, and whom they were waiting for, was Hubert.

Calm down a bit, I thought. Just wait until he has finished

skinning the wolf, and he'll come, believe you me! Then he'll appear over there on the path, the man who can catch Sofia for you!

I burned with shame. I was ashamed that we had a traitor in Cherry Valley. And yet I wanted to see him come, because now at last I would have proof. It was one thing to suspect someone, but now I would know for certain, so that I could say to Sofia:

"That Hubert, get rid of him! Otherwise it'll soon be the end for you and for the whole of Cherry Valley."

How horrible it was, waiting, when there's something horrible to wait for. A traitor is something horrible; I felt that, so that my whole body crawled with it as I lay there. I almost stopped being afraid of the men by the fire because of that awful thing—that I was soon to see the traitor coming on his horse, just where the path came around the cliff. I was terrified at the thought, and yet I stared so that my eyes smarted, toward the place where I knew he would appear.

The two men out by the fire were staring in the same direction. They also knew which way he would come. But none of us knew *when*.

We waited. They waited by their fire and I waited flat on my face in my cave. The moon moved away from the cave entrance, but time, that stood still. Nothing happened, we just waited, waited until I longed to jump up and shout to put an end to it. It was as if everything were waiting, the moon, the mountains roundabout, as if the whole terrible moonlight night was holding its breath, waiting for the traitor.

He came at last. Far away on the path, right in the middle of the moonlight, a rider on his horse was approaching; yes, now I had him exactly where I knew he would appear, and I shuddered when I saw him—Hubert, how could you? I thought.

68

My eyes were smarting so much that I had to close them. Or perhaps I closed them so that I shouldn't see. I had waited so long for this wretch and now that he was actually coming, it was as if I couldn't bear to see his face. So I closed my eyes and just heard from the clump of the horse's hoofs that he was approaching.

At last he arrived and reined in his horse, and then I opened my eyes, for I had to see what a traitor looked like, for he betrayed his own kind; yes, I wanted to see Hubert as he came to betray Cherry Valley and everyone who lived there.

But it wasn't Hubert. It was Jossi! The Golden Cockerel.

CHAPTER EIGHT

JOSSI AND NONE OTHER!

It took me a moment or so to take it in. Jossi, the person who had been so kind and happy and red-cheeked and who had given me cakes and comforted me when I was sad—he was the traitor.

And here he was, sitting by the fire, only a short way away from me, together with those Tengilmen—Veder and Kader, he called them—explaining why he hadn't come earlier.

"Hubert's out hunting wolves in the mountains, and I had to keep out of sight."

Veder and Kader looked sullen, and Jossi went on.

"Surely you haven't forgotten Hubert? You ought to have him in Katla Cavern, too, because he also hates Tengil."

"Then I think you should do something about it," said Veder.

"For you're our man in Cherry Valley, aren't you?" said Kader.

"Of course, of course," said Jossi.

70

He fawned and cringed, but Veder and Kader didn't like him; I could see that. I suppose no one likes a traitor, even if he has his uses.

But he was allowed to keep his ears; they didn't cut them off. But they did something else; they put the Katla mark on him.

"All Tengil's men have to carry the Katla mark, even a traitor like you," said Veder. "So that you can show them who you are, if any spies who don't know you come to Cherry Valley."

"Of course, of course," said Jossi.

They ordered him to open his jacket and shirt, and with a branding iron that they heated in the fire, they burned the Katla mark on to his chest.

Jossi cried out when he was touched by the glowing iron.

"Feel that!" said Kader. "Now you know that for eternity you're one of us, traitor that you are."

Of all the nights in my life, this must have been the longest and hardest, at least since I had come to Nangiyala, and almost the worst of it was having to lie there and listen to Jossi bragging about what he had planned for the destruction of Cherry Valley.

He would soon be able to snare Sofia and Hubert, he said, both of them.

"But that must happen so that no one realizes who lies behind it. Otherwise how could I continue to be your secret Tengilman in Cherry Valley?"

You won't be secret all that much longer, I thought. For here's one person who will expose you, so that you'll turn pale, you red-cheeked wretch, you!

But then he said something else, something that made my heart lurch.

"Have you caught Jonathan Lionheart, yet? Or is he still free in Wild Rose Valley?"

Veder and Kader didn't like the question, I could see. "We're on his tracks," said Veder. "A hundred men are searching for him day and night."

"And we'll find him even if we have to search every single house in Wild Rose Valley," said Kader. "Tengil is waiting for him."

"I can understand that," said Jossi. "Young Lionheart is more dangerous than anyone else, I've told you that. For he is truly a lion."

I felt proud as I lay there that Jonathan was such a lion, and what a comfort it was to know that he was alive. But I wept with rage when I realized what Jossi had done. He had betrayed Jonathan. Only Jossi could have found out about Jonathan's secret journey to Wild Rose Valley and sent a message about it to Tengil. It was Jossi's fault that a hundred men were now searching day and night for my brother and would hand him over to Tengil if they found him.

But he was alive, all the same; he was alive! And he was free too, so why had he called out in my dream? I wondered as I lay there, whether I would ever know.

But I learned a lot of other things by lying there listening to Jossi.

"That Hubert, he's envious of Sofia because we've chosen her as our leader in Cherry Valley," said Jossi. "Because Hubert thinks he's best at everything."

Oh, was that why! I remembered how angry Hubert had sounded that time when he had asked, "What's so special about Sofia?" So it was because he was envious, not for any other reason. You can be envious and still be a good man at the same time. But I had gotten it into my head from the start that Hubert was Cherry Valley's traitor, and everything he had done and said since, I had managed to fit in with that. It was so easy to imagine things wrongly about people. Poor Hubert had watched over me and saved my life and given me smoked meat as well, and in thanks I had only shouted at him: "Don't kill me!" No wonder he was furious. Forgive me, Hubert, I thought, forgive me; I would say that to him if I ever met him again.

Jossi was more assured now, apparently quite pleased as he sat there, but I think the Katla mark stung him sometimes, because he groaned a little every time, and Kader said, "Feel *that*, feel *that*!"

I wished I could have seen what the Katla mark looked like, though it was probably horrible, I imagine, so perhaps it was just as well I didn't see it.

Jossi went on bragging about everything he had done and everything he was going to do, and suddenly he said:

"Lionheart has a little brother, whom he loves above all else."

I wept silently and longed for Jonathan.

"We could use the poor little devil as a bait to get Sofia on the hook," said Jossi.

"You numbskull, why didn't you tell us that before?" said Kader. "We could use the brother, if we had him, to force Lionheart out of his hiding place. For wherever he is hiding, he would certainly find out in some secret way that we had captured his brother."

"And that'd bring him out," said Veder. " 'Free my brother and take me instead,' he'd be bound to say then, if he really cares about his brother and wants to protect him from all evil."

I was so afraid now that I couldn't even cry any more, but Jossi puffed himself out and boasted:

"I'll arrange that when I get back home," he said. "I can lure little Kalle Lionheart into an ambush. That won't be difficult. I can do that with a few cakes. And then we can deceive Sofia into trying to save him."

"Isn't Sofia too clever for you?" said Kader. "Do you think you could deceive her?"

"Oh, yes, yes indeed," said Jossi. "And she won't even know who is doing it. She trusts me."

Now he was so pleased with himself that he chuckled:

"Then you'll have both her and little Lionheart. How many horses will Tengil give me for that when he marches into Cherry Valley?"

That'll be something to see, I thought. Oh, Jossi, so you're going home to lure Kalle Lionheart into an ambush, are you? But if he's no longer in Cherry Valley, what will you do then?

In the middle of all this wretchedness, I was cheered by the thought of how crestfallen Jossi would be when he found out that I had disappeared.

But then Jossi said:

"Little Kalle Lionheart, he's nice, but he's certainly no lion. There's no more easily scared little weakling. Hareheart would be a better name for him."

Yes, I knew myself that I could never be at all brave and that I shouldn't be called Lionheart like Jonathan. But all the same, it was terrible to hear Jossi say it. I felt ashamed as I lay there, and I thought that I must, *must* try to be a little braver, but not just now when I was so afraid.

Jossi at last stopped. He had no more scoundrelly things to boast about, so he got up.

"I must be home before daybreak," he said.

They went on exhorting him until the last moment.

"Make sure you do something about Sofia and that little brother," said Veder.

"Rely on me," said Jossi. "But you mustn't do the boy any harm. Because I care for him a little."

Thank you, I've noticed that, I thought.

74

"And then don't forget the password if you bring news into Wild Rose Valley," said Kader. "If you want to be let in alive!"

"All power to Tengil, our liberator," said Jossi. "No, I remember that day and night. And Tengil, he won't forget his promise to me, will he?"

He had already mounted, ready to leave.

"Jossi, Chieftain of Cherry Valley," he said. "Tengil promised me that I would be that; he won't forget, will he?"

"Tengil forgets nothing," said Kader.

And then Jossi rode away, disappearing the same way he had come, and Veder and Kader sat there watching him go.

"That man," said Veder. "He'll go to Katla when we've finished with Cherry Valley."

He said it so that you knew what it meant to fall into Katla's power. I knew so little about Katla, but I shuddered and almost felt sorry for Jossi, although he was such a wretch.

The fire in the glade had burned low and I began to hope that Veder and Kader would also go away. I wanted it so much that I ached to see them disappear. Like a rat in a trap, I longed to be free. If only I could get their horses out of the cave before someone came in to fetch them, then perhaps I would manage, I thought, and Veder and Kader would ride away without knowing how easily they could have captured Jonathan Lionheart's little brother.

But then I heard Kader say:

"Let's go and sleep in the cave for a while."

Oh, so the end has come, I thought. Well, just as well, for I cannot go on. Let them take me; by all means put an end to it all.

But then Veder said:

"Why sleep? It'll soon be morning and I've had enough of these mountains. I want to go back to Wild Rose Valley now."

So Kader gave in.

"As you like," he said. "Get the horses out."

Sometimes, when things are really dangerous, it's as if you saved yourself without thinking. I threw myself backwards and scrambled into the darkest corner of the cave, just as a little animal might have done. I saw Veder come in through the entrance, but the next moment he was in the pitch-black darkness of the cave and I could see him no longer, only hear him, and that was bad enough. He couldn't see me either, but he ought to have been able to hear my heart. How it thumped as I lay there, waiting for what was to come, when Veder found three horses instead of two.

They whinnied a little when Veder came in. All three, Fyalar too. I would be able to recognize Fyalar's whinny among a thousand others. But Veder, the fool, heard no difference; just imagine, he never even noticed that there were three horses in the cave. He drove out the two nearest to the entrance—their own two—and went after them himself.

As soon as I was alone with Fyalar, I rushed over and put my hand on his nose. Dear, sweet Fyalar, keep quiet, I prayed inwardly, for I knew that if he whinnied now, they would hear out there and realize something was wrong. And Fyalar, he was so clever he understood everything. The other horses whinnied outside, as if they wished to say farewell to him. But Fyalar stood quietly and did not answer.

I saw Veder and Kader mount, and I cannot describe what a wonderful feeling it was. At last I would be free now and out of the rat trap. I thought.

Then Veder said:

"I've forgotten my tinderbox."

And he jumped down from his horse and began to search around the fire.

Then he said:

"It isn't here. Perhaps I dropped it in the cave."

That was how the rat trap closed on me again with a crash, and I was caught. Veder came into the cave to look for that wretched tinderbox and he walked straight into Fyalar.

I know that one shouldn't lie, but if it's a matter of life and death, you have to.

He had hard hands, too, Veder had; no one has ever held me so roughly before. It hurt and I was angry, almost more angry than afraid, strangely enough. Perhaps that's why I lied so well.

"How long have you been lying here spying?" bawled Veder as he dragged me out of the cave.

"Since last night," I said. "But I was only sleeping," I said, blinking in the morning light as if I'd just woken up.

"Sleeping," said Veder. "Are you trying to tell me that you never heard us bellowing and singing out here by the fire? Don't lie now."

He thought that was being very cunning, for they hadn't sung a single note. But I was even more cunning.

"Well, perhaps I heard a *little* when you were singing," I stammered, as if I were lying to please him.

Then Veder and Kader looked at each other; now they knew for certain that I'd been asleep and hadn't heard a thing.

But that didn't help all that much.

"Don't you know it's the death penalty for traveling this way?" said Veder.

I tried to look as if I didn't know anything about anything: not a thing about the death penalty or anything else.

"I only wanted to see the moonlight last night," I mumbled.

"And you risked your life for that, you little fox?" said Veder. "Where do you live, in Cherry Valley or in Wild Rose Valley?"

"In Wild Rose Valley," I said.

Because Karl Lionheart lived in Cherry Valley and I would rather die than tell them who I was.

"Who are your parents?" asked Veder.

"I live with . . . with my grandfather," I said.

"What's his name?" said Veder.

"I just call him Grandfather," I said, making myself out to be even stupider.

"Where does he live in Wild Rose Valley?" said Veder.

"In a . . . little white house," I said, for I thought that the houses in Wild Rose Valley would probably be white, as they are in Cherry Valley.

"You can show us that grandfather and that white house," said Veder. "Up on that horse with you."

So we rode away and just then the sun rose behind Nangiyala's mountains. The sky was ablaze with burning fire and the mountain peaks were shining. I have never in my whole life seen anything more beautiful, anything more colossal, and if I hadn't had Kader and the black rump of his horse straight in front of me, I would have been jubilant. But I wasn't, no, indeed I wasn't.

The path continued to twist and turn just as before, but soon it ran steeply downhill and I realized that we were approaching Wild Rose Valley. Yet I could scarcely believe it when I suddenly saw it right below me; oh, it was as beautiful as Cherry Valley, lying there in the morning light with its small houses and farms and its green slopes and flowering wild-rose thickets; whole drifts of wild roses, there were. It looked so odd from above, almost like a sea with pink foam on the green waves; yes, Wild Rose Valley was the right name for such a valley.

But I would never have gotten into that valley without Veder and Kader, for there was a high wall, which Tengil had forced the people to build because he wanted them as bondsmen, imprisoned for ever. Jonathan had told me that, so I knew.

Veder and Kader must have forgotten to ask me how I had managed to get out of the closed valley, and I prayed to God that they would never remember to either. For what could I answer? How could anyone get over that wall—and with a horse as well?

Tengilmen in black helmets and with swords and spears were on guard on the top of the wall as far as I could see, and the gateway was just as well guarded; there was a gateway in the wall just where the path from Cherry Valley came to an end.

Here people had traveled freely between the valleys for centuries and now there was nothing but a closed gate and you had to be a Tengilman to get through.

Veder thundered on the gate with his sword. Then a little shutter opened and a giantlike man stuck his head out.

"Password!" he cried.

Veder and Kader whispered the secret passwords into his ear, no doubt so that I shouldn't hear. But that was unnecessary, because I knew the words too—"All power to Tengil, our liberator."

The man behind the shutter looked at me and said:

"And him? Who's he?"

"It's a little oaf we found up in the mountains," said Kader. "But he can't be all that stupid, because he somehow managed to get through your gate last night,—what do you say to that, Senior Guard? I think you should ask your men how they keep guard in the evenings."

The man behind the shutter grew angry. He opened the gate, but he scolded and swore and was reluctant to let me in, only Veder and Kader.

"Put him in Katla Cavern," he said. "He belongs there."

But Veder and Kader were stubborn—I *must* be allowed in, they said, because I must prove that I hadn't lied to them. It was their duty to Tengil to find that out, they said.

And with Veder and Kader as escorts, I rode through the gate.

I thought then that if I ever saw Jonathan again, I would tell him how Veder and Kader had helped me into Wild Rose Valley. He would laugh about that for a long time.

But I was not laughing, because I knew how bad things were for me. I had to find a white house with a grandfather in it; otherwise I would end up in Katla Cavern.

"Ride on ahead and show us the way," said Veder. "For we must speak seriously to your grandfather."

There were plenty of white houses, just like at home in Cherry Valley, but I didn't see one that I could point out, because I didn't know who lived in them. I didn't dare say "Grandfather lives there," for suppose Veder and Kader went in and there was not even one little old man there, not one who wanted to be grandfather to me.

Now I was truly in a mess and I sweated as I rode along. It had been so easy to invent a grandfather, but now I no longer thought it such a good idea.

I saw people working outside their houses, but nowhere anyone who resembled a grandfather, and I began to feel more and more miserable. It was terrible, too, to see how things were with the people in Wild Rose Valley, how pale and hungry and unhappy they all were, at least those I saw as I rode along, so unlike the people of Cherry Valley. But then we had no Tengil in our valley, who enslaved us and took from us everything we had to live on.

I rode and rode, and Veder and Kader began to get impatient, but I just rode on as if I were on my way to the end of the world.

"Is it much farther?" said Veder.

"No, not far," I said, but I didn't know what I was saying or doing. Now I was terrified, just waiting to be thrown into Katla Cavern.

But then a miracle happened. Believe it or not, outside a little white house an old man was sitting on a bench just by the wall, feeding his pigeons. Perhaps I would never have dared do it if there hadn't been one snow-white pigeon in among all those gray ones. Just one!

Tears came into my eyes; I had seen pigeons like that only at Sofia's and then once on my windowsill long ago, in another world.

Then I did an unheard-of thing. I jumped down from Fyalar and in two leaps, I was with the old man. I threw myself into his arms and with my arms around his neck, I whispered in my despair:

"Help me! Save me! Say that you are my grandfather!"

I was frightened and sure that he would push me away when he saw Veder and Kader in their black helmets behind me. Why should he lie for my sake and perhaps end up in Katla Cavern because of it?

But he didn't push me away. He held me tight and I felt his good, kind arms around me like a protection against all evil.

"Little lad," he said, so loudly that Veder and Kader could hear him. "Where have you been all this time? And what have you done, unhappy child, to return home with soldiers?"

My poor grandfather, what a scolding he got from Veder and Kader! They scolded and scolded and said that if he didn't keep his grandchildren in better order, but let them roam about in Nangiyala's mountains, then soon he would have no grandchild left, and he would never forget it. But they would let it go for this time, they said at last, and then they rode away. Their helmets could soon be seen as nothing but small black dots on the hillside below us.

Then I began to cry. I was still in my grandfather's arms and I just cried and cried, for the night had been so long and hard and now at last it was over. And my grandfather, he let me, just rocking me a little, and I wished, oh, how I wished he could be my real grandfather. I tried to tell him that although I was crying.

"Well, I can probably be your grandfather," he said. "But otherwise my name is Mathias. What's yours?"

"Karl Lio—" I began. But then I stopped. How could I be so foolish as to say that name here in Wild Rose Valley?

"Grandfather dear, my name is a secret," I said. "Call me Rusky."

"Oh, Rusky, is it?" said Mathias, laughing a little. "Go on into the kitchen, Rusky, and wait for me there," he went on. "I'll just put your horse in the stable."

I went in, into a poor little kitchen with nothing but a table and a wooden sofa and a few chairs and a hearth. There was also a big sideboard along one wall.

Mathias soon came back, and then I said:

"We've got a big sideboard like that in our kitchen, too, at home in Cher—"

Then I stopped.

"At home in Cherry Valley," said Mathias, and I looked anxiously at him—once again I had said what mustn't be said.

But Mathias said nothing else. He went over to the window and looked out, standing there for a long time, looking about as if he wanted to be sure that there was no one around. Then he turned to me and said in a low voice:

"Though there's something special about that sideboard. Wait a minute, and you'll see."

He put his shoulder against the sideboard and pushed it aside. Behind it was a shutter in the wall. He opened it and inside there was a room, a very small room. Someone was lying asleep on the floor.

It was Jonathan.

CHAPTER NINE

I CAN REMEMBER A FEW TIMES WHEN I HAVE been so happy that I have hardly known what to do with myself; once, when I was small and for Christmas Jonathan gave me a toboggan that he had been saving up for a long time. Then that time when I first came to Nangiyala and found Jonathan down by the stream, and the whole of that amazing evening at Knights Farm when I was so happy I could hardly contain myself. But nothing, *nothing* could compare with finding Jonathan on the floor at Mathias's place; think, that one can be so happy! It was as if I were laughing aloud in my very soul.

I didn't touch Jonathan. I didn't wake him. I didn't cry out with joy or go wild. I just lay down beside him quietly and fell asleep.

How long did I sleep? I don't know. All day, I think. But when I woke up—yes, when I woke up, Jonathan was sitting on the floor beside me. He was just sitting there smiling; no one looks as kind as Jonathan when he smiles. I had thought that perhaps he wouldn't be all that pleased that I had come, that he had perhaps already forgotten he had called for help. But now I could see that he was just as pleased as I was. So I had to smile, I too, and we sat there just looking at each other, saying nothing for a while.

"You called for help," I said at last.

Then Jonathan stopped smiling.

"Why did you call?" I said.

It was clearly something he could not think about without being upset. His reply came so quietly it was as if he could hardly bear to answer me.

"I saw Katla," he said. "I saw what Katla did."

I didn't want to torment him with questions about Katla, and anyhow I had so much to tell him, first and foremost about Jossi.

Jonathan didn't really want to believe it. His face turned white and he almost wept.

"Jossi, no, no, not Jossi," he said, tears coming into his eyes.

But then he rushed up.

"Sofia must be told at once."

"How can we do that?" I said.

"One of her pigeons is here," he said. "Bianca. She can fly back this evening."

Yes, Sofia's pigeon, I thought so! I told him that it was because of that pigeon that I was there with him and not in Katla's Cavern.

"It was a miracle," I said, "that among all the houses in Wild Rose Valley I should come straight to the one you were in. But if Bianca hadn't been outside, I would have ridden past."

"Bianca, Bianca, thank you for sitting there," said Jonathan. But he had no time to listen to me any more; haste was important now. He scratched on the shutter with his fingernails, rather like a little mouse scratching, and it wasn't long before the shutter opened and Mathias peered in.

"And little Rusky, he just goes on and on sleeping . . ." Mathias began, but Jonathan wouldn't let him continue.

"Please get Bianca," he said. "She must leave as soon as dusk begins to fall."

He explained why, telling Mathias about Jossi. Mathias shook his head in that way old people do when they are sad.

"Jossi! I knew it must be someone from Cherry Valley," he said. "And that's why Orvar is in Katla Cavern now. My God, the people there are in this world."

Then he vanished to fetch Bianca, closing the shutter on us.

It was a good hiding place Jonathan had with Mathias, a tiny secret chamber with neither window nor door; the only way in was through the shutter behind the sideboard. There was no furniture in it, only a feather mattress to sleep on, and an old horn lamp which dispelled the darkness in there a little.

In the light of this lamp, Jonathan wrote a message to Sofia. "The name of the traitor, who shall be cursed forever, is Jossi the Golden Cockerel. Get him quickly. My brother is here now."

"That was why Bianca came flying in yesterday evening," said Jonathan. "To tell us that you had disappeared and had gone to find me."

"Just think, that means Sofia understood the puzzle I wrote on the kitchen wall," I said. "When she came with the soup."

"What puzzle?" said Jonathan.

"I've gone to find him far, far away beyond the mountains."

I told him what I had written.

"I did it so that Sofia wouldn't be worried," I said.

Jonathan laughed.

"Not be worried—that's what you think. And me? How calm do you think I was when I learned that you were some-where up in the mountains of Nangiyala!"

I must have looked ashamed, because he hastened to comfort me.

"Brave little Rusky, it's wonderful that you were there all the same, and even more wonderful that you are here."

That was the first time anyone had ever called me brave and I thought that if I went on in this way, then perhaps I would be able to call myself Lionheart, despite Jossi.

But then I remembered what else I had written on the wall at home, about someone with a red beard who wanted white horses. I asked Jonathan to add a line to the message:

"Karl says all that about red beard is wrong."

I also told him how Hubert had saved me from the wolves and Jonathan said that he would be grateful to him for the rest of his life.

Dusk was falling over Wild Rose Valley as we went to release Bianca, and lights began to go on in all the houses and farms on the slope below us. It looked so calm and peaceful that you might have thought people were now sitting down eating their good evening meal or perhaps just talking to each other and playing with their children or singing little songs to them and enjoying life. But you knew it wasn't like that. You knew that they had hardly anything to eat and that they weren't calm and happy, only unhappy. Tengilmen up on the wall with their swords and spears helped you to remember how things were, in case you might forget.

There were no lights in Mathias's windows. His house was dark, and everything was silent, as if there weren't a living soul in it. But we were there, not in the house, but outside, Mathias standing guard at the corner of the house, and Jonathan and I crawling among the wild roses with Bianca.

There were thickets like that all round Mathias's place, and wild roses are something I like, for they smell so sweet, not strong, just sweet. But I thought to myself that I would never again be able to smell the scent of wild roses without my heart thumping, and remembering how we crept among the bushes, Jonathan and I, so close to the wall, where Tengilmen were listening and watching, perhaps most of all for someone with the name of Lionheart.

Jonathan had blackened his face and pulled a hood right down over his eyes. He didn't look like Jonathan, I must say. But it was dangerous all the same, and he was risking his life every time he left his hiding place in the secret chamber, his hideout, as he called it. A hundred men were searching for him day and night, I knew, and I had told him so, but all he said was:

"Yes, they can carry on doing that, I think."

He had to release Bianca himself, he said, because he wanted to be certain that no one saw her as she flew away.

The guards on the wall seemed to have a piece of it each to guard. There was a fat one patrolling up and down all the time on the top of the wall just behind Mathias's place, and we had to watch out for him.

But Mathias was standing at the corner of the house with his horn lamp, and he arranged with us how he would signal. This is what he said:

"When I hold the lamp down low, then you mustn't even breathe, for then Fatty Dodik is quite close. But when I hold the lamp up high, then he's over where the wall curves away and he usually talks to another Tengilman there. That's when you must let Bianca go."

And that's what we did.

"Fly, fly," said Jonathan. "Fly, my Bianca, over the mountains of Nangiyala to Cherry Valley. And watch out for Jossi's arrows."

I don't know whether Sofia's pigeons really understood human speech, but I think perhaps Bianca did, because she laid her beak against Jonathan's cheek as if wishing to calm him and then she flew away. She glimmered white in the dusk, so danger- ously white. How easily Dodik could have seen her as she went flying over the wall.

But he didn't. He was probably standing there talking, neither seeing nor hearing anything. Mathias was keeping watch, and he did not lower the lamp.

We saw Bianca disappear and I pulled at Jonathan because I wanted him to go quickly back to the hiding place. But Jonathan didn't want to. Not yet. It was such a lovely evening, the air cool and pleasant to breathe. He had no desire to creep back into a stuffy little room. No one could understand that better than I, who had lain for so long shut in the kitchen at home in town.

Jonathan was sitting in the grass with his arms around his knees, looking down toward the valley quite calmly. One might have thought that he was considering sitting there all evening, however many Tengilmen were patrolling the wall behind him.

"Why are you sitting there?" I said.

"Because I like it," said Jonathan. "Because I like this valley at dusk. And the cool air on my face—I like that too. And wild pink roses that smell of summer."

"So do I," I said.

"And I like flowers and grass and trees and fields and forests and beautiful small lakes," said Jonathan. "And when the sun rises and when the sun sets and when the moon is out and the stars twinkle and a few other things that I can't remember at the moment."

"I like those things too."

"Everyone likes them," said Jonathan. "And if that's all people ask for, can you tell me why they can't have peace and quiet without a Tengil coming along and destroying every-thing?"

I couldn't answer that. Then Jonathan said:

"Come on, we'd better go in."

But we couldn't just run straight back in, because first we had to know how things were back with Mathias and where Fatty was.

It had grown dark. You couldn't see Mathias any longer, only the light from the lamp.

"He's holding it up high. No Dodik there," said Jonathan. "Come on."

But just as we began to run, the light from the lamp sank like lightning and we had to stop suddenly. We heard horses approaching at a gallop and then how they slowed down and someone spoke to Mathias.

Jonathan gave me a little nudge in the back.

"Go on," he whispered. "Go over to Mathias."

Then he threw himself straight into a wild rose thicket, and trembling and afraid, I walked toward the lamplight.

"I just wanted a bit of air," I heard Mathias saying. "It's such lovely weather this evening."

"Lovely weather," replied a rough voice. "There's the death penalty for being out after sunset, didn't you know that?"

"A disobedient old grandfather, that's what you are," said another voice. "Where's the boy, anyway?"

"He's just coming," said Mathias. I was now quite near him, and I recognized those two on the horses, I did. It was Veder and Kader.

"Are you off up into the mountains to look at the moonlight tonight, then?" said Veder. "What was your name, now, you little rascal? I didn't catch it."

"I'm just called Rusky," I said. I dared say that, because no one knew that name, neither Jossi nor anyone else, only Jonathan and I and Mathias.

"Rusky, indeed," said Kader. "Now listen, Rusky, why do you think we've come here?"

I felt as if my legs would give way beneath me.

To put me into Katla Cavern, I thought. They must have regretted letting me go, of course, and now they had come to fetch me. What else?

"Well, you see," said Kader. "We ride around this valley in the evenings to see that people are obeying what Tengil has decided. But your grandfather finds it hard to grasp; perhaps you could explain to him how bad it would be for both of you if you don't stay indoors after dark."

"And don't forget," said Veder. "You won't escape a second time if we find you where you shouldn't be; remember that, Rusky. If your grandfather lives or dies, it's all the same to us. But you, you are so young, you want to grow up and become a Tengilman, don't you?"

A Tengilman, no, I'd rather die, I thought, but I didn't say so. I was terribly anxious about Jonathan and I dared not annoy them, so I answered very meekly:

"Yes, I do."

"Good," said Veder. "Then you can go down to the big landing stage early tomorrow morning and you'll be able to see Tengil, the liberator of Wild Rose Valley. Tomorrow he is crossing the river of The Ancient Rivers in his golden sloop and is disembarking at the big landing stage."

Then they prepared to leave, but Kader reined in his horse at the last moment.

"Listen, old man!" he shouted at Mathias, who was already halfway to the house. "You haven't seen a handsome fair-haired youth called Lionheart anywhere, have you?"

91

I was holding Mathias's hand and I felt how he trembled, but he answered calmly:

"I know no Lionheart."

"Oh, don't you?" said Kader. "But if you happen to meet him, then you know what happens to anyone who gives him shelter or hides him? The death penalty, you know?"

Then Mathias closed the door behind us.

"Death penalties here and death penalties there," he said. "That's all those people think about."

The sound of horses' hoofs had hardly died away when Mathias was out with the lamp again. Jonathan soon appeared, his hands and face badly scratched by thorns but glad that nothing worse had happened and that Bianca was now in full flight over the mountains.

Later on, we had our evening meal in the kitchen at Mathias's, with the shutter open so that Jonathan could quickly disappear into his hiding place if anyone came.

But first we went out to the stable, Jonathan and I, and fed our horses. It was wonderful to see them again, standing with their heads close together. I suppose they were telling each other about everything that had happened. I gave both of them some oats. At first, Jonathan tried to stop me, but then he said:

"Yes, let them have some for once. But you don't give oats to *horses* any longer here in Wild Rose Valley."

When we went into the kitchen, Mathias had put a bowl of soup on the table.

"We haven't anything else, and it's mostly water," he said. "But at least it's hot."

I looked around for my sack, remembering what was in it, and when I pulled out all my loaves and my smoked meat, both Jonathan and Mathias gasped, and their eyes began to shine. It was a marvelous feeling to have what was almost a feast to offer them. I cut thick slices of meat and we ate soup and bread and

92

smoked meat; we ate and ate and ate. No one said anything, not for a long while, then at last Jonathan said:

"Oh, to have had enough to eat! I'd almost forgotten what it was like to be full."

I became more and more pleased that I had come to Wild Rose Valley; it felt more and more right and good. Then I had to tell them properly about everything that had happened to me from the moment I had ridden away from home until Veder and Kader had helped me into Wild Rose Valley. I had already told them most of it, but Jonathan wanted to hear it several times, especially about Veder and Kader. He laughed about that, just as I had thought he would. And Mathias did too.

"They're not all that bright, those Tengilmen," said Mathias. "Although they think they are."

"No, even I could trick them," I said. "Just think if they'd known that the little brother they wanted to get hold of so much was the very one they'd helped into Wild Rose Valley and let go just like that."

When I had said it, I began to think. I hadn't thought about it before, but now I asked:

"However did you get into Wild Rose Valley, Jonathan?"

Jonathan laughed.

"I leapt my way in."

"What do you mean leapt . . . surely not with Grim?"

"Yes," said Jonathan. "I haven't any other horse."

I had seen and knew what great leaps Jonathan could do on Grim, but to leap over the wall around Wild Rose Valley was more than any human being could believe.

"You see, the wall wasn't quite finished then," said Jonathan. "Not everywhere. Not to its full height, though it was high enough, you can be sure of that."

"Yes, but the guards!" I said. "Did no one see you?"

Jonathan took a bite of bread, then laughed again.

"Yes, I had a whole swarm of them after me, and Grim got an arrow in his rump. But I got away, and a kind peasant hid both Grim and me in his barn. And that night he brought me here to Mathias. Now you know everything."

"No, you don't know everything at all," said Mathias. "You don't know that the people here in the valley sing songs about that ride and about Jonathan. His coming here is the only good thing that has happened in Wild Rose Valley since Tengil invaded us and made us bondsmen. 'Jonathan our savior' they sing, because he's going to liberate Wild Rose Valley, believe you me; I believe that too. Now you know everything."

"You don't know everything at all," said Jonathan. "You don't know that Mathias is the one who is leading the secret struggle in Wild Rose Valley, now that Orvar is in Katla Cavern. They should call Mathias the savior, not me."

"No, I'm too old," said Mathias. "He's so right, that Veder. It's all the same whether I live or die."

"You mustn't say that," I said. "Because you're my grandfather."

"Well, then, that's what I shall stay alive for. But I'm not fit to lead a struggle any longer. You have to be young for that."

He sighed.

"If only Orvar were here. But he's in Katla Cavern, until he's given to Katla."

I saw that Jonathan's face had turned quite white.

"We'll see," he mumbled. "We'll see whom Katla gets in the end."

But then he said:

"Now we must set to work. You don't know either, Rusky, that here in this cottage, we sleep in the daytime and work at night. Come on, and I'll show you."

He crawled ahead of me through the shutter into the hideout, and there he showed me something. He threw aside the feather

94

mattress which we had slept on and took up two wide loose floorboards under it.

There I saw a black hole going straight down into the earth.

"This is where my underground passage starts," said Jonathan.

"And where does it end?" I asked, though I could almost guess what his reply would be.

"In the wild country on the other side of the wall," he said. "It'll come up there when it's finished. A couple more nights and then I think it'll be long enough."

He crept down into the hole.

"But I must dig a bit farther," he said. "For you must see that I don't want to pop up right under Fatty Dodik's nose."

Then he vanished and I sat there waiting for a long time. When he came back at last, he was pushing a trough full of earth in front of him. He heaved it up to me and I dragged it through the shutter to Mathias.

"More earth for my field," said Mathias. "If only I had a few peas and beans to sow and plant there, that would be the end of our hunger."

"Do you think so?" said Jonathan. "Tengil takes nine out of every ten beans in your field; have you forgotten that?"

"You're right," said Mathias. "So long as Tengil is alive, there'll be hunger and need in Wild Rose Valley."

Mathias was now going to sneak out and empty the trough on his field, and I was told to stay by the door and keep watch. I was to whistle, said Jonathan, if I noticed the slightest thing that might be dangerous. A special little tune, I was to whistle, one that Jonathan had taught me a long time ago when we lived on earth. We used to whistle a lot together at that time, in the evenings after we had gone to bed. So I've always been able to whistle.

Jonathan crawled down into his hole again to go on digging,

and Mathias closed the shutter and pushed back the sideboard.

"Get this into your head, Rusky," he said. "Never, never let Jonathan be in there without the shutter being closed and the sideboard pushed across. Get it into your head that you're in a country where Tengil lives and rules."

"I won't forget," I said.

It was dim in the kitchen, a single candle burning on the table, but Mathias put it out.

"The night must be dark in Wild Rose Valley," he said. "For there are so many eyes wanting to see what they shouldn't see."

Then he took the trough and vanished, and I stood at the open door to keep watch. It was dark, just as Mathias wanted it to be. It was dark in the houses, and the sky over Wild Rose Valley was dark too, no stars twinkling and no moon. I could see nothing at all. But all those eyes of the night that Mathias had talked about, they couldn't see anything either, I thought, and that was a comfort.

I felt miserable and lonely, standing there waiting, and it was creepy, too. Mathias was taking so long. I grew uneasy, more and more uneasy every moment that went by. Why didn't he come? I stared out into the darkness. But it wasn't quite so dark now, was it? Suddenly I thought that it had grown lighter. Or was it only my eyes getting used to it? Then I saw what it was. The moon was coming out through the clouds, which was the worst thing that could happen, and I prayed to God that Mathias would get back in time while it was still dark enough to hide him. But it was too late, for now the moon was shining brilliantly and a river of moonlight was flooding the valley.

I saw Mathias in that light; far away, I saw him coming through the thickets with his trough. I looked wildly around, for I was supposed to be keeping watch, and then I saw something else, too—Dodik, Fatty Dodik, climbing down the wall on a rope ladder, his back to me.

It's very difficult to whistle when you're frightened, so it didn't sound too good, but I more or less managed to get that tune out, and as swiftly as a lizard, Mathias vanished behind the nearest wild rose thicket.

By then Dodik was already upon me.

"What are you whistling for?" he shouted.

"Because—because I learned to today," I stammered. "I couldn't whistle before, but just think, I can suddenly do it today. Do you want to hear me?"

I started whistling again but Dodik stopped me.

"No, shut up, now," he said. "Not that I know whether it's forbidden to whistle, but I expect it is. I don't think Tengil likes it. And anyhow you should keep your door shut, you know."

"Doesn't Tengil like you leaving your door open?" I said.

"Mind your own business," said Dodik. "Do as you're told. But give me a ladle of water first. I'm dying of thirst up there on that wall."

I thought quickly; if he comes after me into the kitchen and finds Mathias isn't there, what'll happen? Poor Mathias, the death sentence for being out at night; I'd heard enough about that.

"I'll get some," I said quickly. "Stay here and I'll get you some water."

I ran inside and in the dark fumbled my way to the water barrel. I knew which corner it was in. I found the ladle, too, and filled it with water. Then I felt someone standing behind me; yes, he was standing there in the darkness just behind my back, and I've rarely felt anything so creepy.

"Light the candle," said Dodik. "I want to see what this kind of rat hole looks like."

My hands shook; I was shaking all over, but I managed to light the candle all the same.

Dodik took the ladle and drank. He drank and drank as if he were a bottomless pit. Then he flung the ladle down on the floor and looked around suspiciously with his horrible little eyes. Then he asked just what I had expected him to ask.

"That old Mathias who lives here, where is he?"

I didn't answer. I didn't know what to answer.

"Didn't you hear what I said?" said Dodik. "Where's Mathias?"

"He's asleep," I said. I had to think up something.

"Where?"

There was a little room off the kitchen and Mathias had his bed in there, I knew, but I also knew he wasn't asleep in there now. I pointed toward the door and said:

"In there."

I squeaked it out, almost inaudibly. It sounded feeble and Dodik laughed mockingly at me.

"You don't lie very well," he said. "Wait while I look."

He was so pleased, knowing that I had lied, and I expect he wanted to arrange Mathias's death sentence and perhaps be praised by Tengil.

"Give me the candle," he said, and I gave it to him. I wanted to rush away, just bolt out of the door and get hold of Mathias and tell him to flee before it was too late. But I couldn't move from the spot. I just stood there, feeling sick with fear.

Dodik saw this and enjoyed the sight. He was in no hurry; oh no, he grinned and dallied just to frighten me more than ever. But when he had stopped grinning, he said:

"Come on, lad, just show me where old Mathias is lying asleep."

He kicked open the door of the room and pushed me so hard that I tripped over the high step. Then he jerked me up again and stood in front of me with the candle in his hand.

"You liar, show me, now," he said, raising the candle to light up the room.

I didn't dare move or look up; I would have liked to dissolve into nothing, I was so desperate.

But then, in the middle of my misery, I heard Mathias's angry voice:

"What's going on? Can't a man even sleep in peace at night?"

I looked up and saw Mathias; yes, he was sitting there in his bed in the dimmest corner of the room, peering at the light. He was wearing only a shirt and his hair was untidy, as if he had been asleep for a long time. Over by the window was the trough, leaning against the wall. This grandfather of mine must indeed have been as quick as a lizard.

I felt almost sorry for Dodik. I've never seen anyone look so utterly stupid as he did, as he stood there glaring at Mathias.

"I only came for a little water," he said sullenly.

"Water, oh yes, that's a good one," said Mathias. "Don't you know that Tengil has forbidden you to take water from us? He thinks we'll poison you. And if you come and wake me up again, I will, too."

I don't know how he dared talk like that to Dodik, but perhaps that's the right way to speak to a Tengilman, for Dodik just grunted and disappeared out to his wall.

CHAPTER TEN

*I*HAD NEVER SEEN A REALLY CRUEL PERSON UNTIL I SAW
Tengil of Karmanyaka.

He came across the river of The Ancient Rivers in his golden
sloop and I was standing there waiting with Mathias.

It was Jonathan who had sent me. He wanted me to see
Tengil.

"Because then you'll understand better why people here in
the valley toil and starve and die with but one thought and one
dream—to see their valley free again."

High up in the mountains of The Ancient Mountains, Tengil
had his castle. He lived there, only occasionally crossing the
river to Wild Rose Valley to strike terror into the people, so that
no one would forget who he was or begin to dream too much
about freedom, Jonathan said.

At first I could hardly see anything, because there were so
many Tengil soldiers in front of me, rows of them, to protect
Tengil while he was in Wild Rose Valley. He was afraid, I
suppose, while he was in Wild Rose Valley, that an arrow

might come whistling out of some hidden corner. Tyrants are always afraid, Jonathan had said, and Tengil was the worst of all tyrants.

No, at first we could see nothing, neither Mathias nor I, but then I found out what to do. They stood there so cocksure, and with their feet wide apart, Tengil's soldiers, that if I lay down flat on my stomach behind the one with his legs farthest apart, I could see through them.

But I couldn't get Mathias to do that.

"The main thing is that you see," he said. "And that you never forget what you see today."

And I saw—a beautiful great gilded boat coming toward us out on the river, black-clad men at the oars. There were a lot of oars, more than I could count, and the blades flashed in the sun each time they were raised out of the water. The oarsmen had to work hard, for there were strong currents pulling at the boat. Perhaps it was the suction from a waterfall farther down the river, for I could hear the thunder of mighty waters far away.

"That's Karma Falls that you can hear," said Mathias, when I asked him. "The song of Karma Falls. That's our cradle song here in Wild Rose Valley, which the children lie and listen to before they go to sleep."

I thought about the children of Wild Rose Valley. They must have run about and played and splashed and had fun down here by the riverbank before. Now they couldn't because of the wall, that dreadful wall which enclosed everything. There were only two gates through the whole length of the wall, the one that I had come through, called the main gateway, and then another here by the river, with a landing stage outside it, where Tengil's sloop was now moored. The gate had been opened for Tengil, and through the archway and between a soldier's legs, I saw the landing stage and Tengil's black stallion waiting there, a fine horse with its saddle gleaming with gold and its harness gleaming with gold. And I saw Tengil step forward and swing himself up into the saddle and come riding through the gateway. Suddenly he was quite close to me and I saw his cruel face and his cruel eyes. Cruel as a serpent, Jonathan had said, and that's what he looked like, cruel through and through and bloodthirsty, too. The costume he was wearing was as red as blood, and the plumes on his helmet were also red, as if he had dipped them in blood. His eyes stared straight ahead; he did not look at the people, just as if there were nothing else in the whole world except Tengil of Karmanyaka; yes, he was terrible.

Everyone in Wild Rose Valley had been ordered to come to the village square, where Tengil was going to speak to them. Mathias and I went there too, of course.

It was such a fine and pretty little square, with beautiful old houses all around it, and there Tengil had them all now, all the people of Wild Rose Valley, exactly as he had ordered. They were standing quietly, just waiting, but oh, how you could feel their bitterness and sorrow. Here in this square they must have enjoyed life before, perhaps danced and played and sung on summer evenings, or perhaps just sat on a bench outside the inn and talked to each other under the lime trees.

Two old lime trees grew there, and Tengil had ridden up and placed himself in between them. He remained mounted and stared out over the square and the people, but he did not see a single one of them, I'm certain. He had his chief adviser beside him, a proud man called Pyuke, Mathias told me. Pyuke had a white horse almost as fine as Tengil's black one, and they sat there like two potentates on their horses, just staring straight ahead. They sat like that for a long time. The soldiers stood around them, on guard, Tengilmen in black helmets and black cloaks, their swords drawn. You could see that they were sweating, for the sun was already high in the sky and it was a hot day.

"What do you think Tengil will say?" I asked Mathias.

"That he's dissatisfied with us," said Mathias. "He never says anything else."

Tengil didn't actually speak himself. He wouldn't speak to bondsmen. He just spoke to Pyuke and then Pyuke had to proclaim how dissatisfied Tengil was with the people of Wild Rose Valley. They didn't work hard enough and they protected Tengil's enemies.

"Lionheart has still not been found," said Pyuke. "Our gracious sovereign is dissatisfied with that."

"Yes, I can see that, I can see that," I heard someone mumble just beside me. There was a poor man standing there, dressed in rags, a little old man with tangled hair and a tangled gray beard.

"Our gracious sovereign's patience is almost at an end," said Pyuke, "and he will punish Wild Rose Valley severely, without mercy."

"Yes, he's right there, he's right there," whined the old man beside me, and I realized he must be a simpleton, not quite right in the head.

"But," said Pyuke, "in his great goodness, our gracious sovereign will wait a while longer before issuing his punishment, and he has even offered a reward. Twenty white horses will be given to the person who captures Lionheart for him."

"Then I'll get the little fox," said the old man, nudging me in the side. "Twenty white horses I'll get from our gracious sovereign; oh, that's good payment for a little fox like that."

I was so angry I would have liked to hit him; even if he was a simpleton, he was talking stupidly.

"Have you no sense?" I whispered, and then he laughed.

"No, not much," he said. Then he looked straight at me and I saw his eyes; Jonathan was the only person in the world with such beautiful shining eyes.

104

It was true, he really did have no sense. How could he have the nerve to come here right under Tengil's nose! Though of course, no one would recognize him. Not even Mathias did, until Jonathan slapped him on the back and said:

"Old man, haven't we met before?"

Jonathan liked dressing up. He used to playact for me in the kitchen in the evenings, when we lived on earth, I mean. He could make a real fright of himself and be so funny that I laughed so much sometimes my stomach used to ache.

But now, here, in front of Tengil, it was almost too bold.

"I must see what happens, too," he whispered, and he wasn't laughing then, for there was nothing to laugh at, either.

For Tengil made all the men of Wild Rose Valley stand in a row in front of him, and with his cruel forefinger, he pointed out which of them were to be taken across the river to Karmanyaka. I knew what that meant, for Jonathan had told me. None of those whom Tengil pointed out would ever come back alive. They would have to toil in Karmanyaka and haul stones up to the fortress which Tengil was having built on the top of the mountains of The Ancient Mountains. A fortress that could never be conquered by an enemy, it was to be, and there Tengil was to sit in his cruelty, year in and year out, and at last feel safe. But a great many bondsmen went into building such a fortress, and they had to toil until they fell.

"And then Katla gets them," Jonathan had said. When I remembered that, I shuddered in the warm sunlight. Katla was still only a horrible name to me then, nothing more.

It was quiet in the square while Tengil was pointing, only a little bird high up in the top of a tree above him singing and trilling beautifully, unaware of what Tengil was doing down there under the lime trees.

Then there was the weeping, too. It was pitiable to hear how they wept, all the women who would lose their husbands and all the children who would never see their fathers again. Everyone wept; I too.

Tengil did not hear the weeping; he just sat on his horse and pointed and pointed and the diamond on his forefinger flashed every time he condemned someone to death. It was terrible; he condemned people to death with nothing but his forefinger.

But one of the men he pointed at must have gone mad when he heard his children crying, for suddenly he broke out of the line, and before the soldiers could stop him, he had rushed up to Tengil.

"Tyrant!" he shouted. "One day you'll die, too, have you thought about that!"

And then he spat on Tengil.

Tengil did not move a muscle. He just made a sign with his hand and the soldier nearest raised his sword. I saw it flashing in the sunlight, but just then Jonathan grasped the back of my neck and pressed me to his chest, hiding my face, so that I saw no more. But I felt, or perhaps I heard, the sobs in Jonathan's breast, and as we walked home, he was weeping, which he never does usually.

They grieved in Wild Rose Valley that day. Everyone grieved. Everyone except Tengil's soldiers. On the contrary, they were pleased every time Tengil came to Wild Rose Valley, for then he gave all his Tengilmen a feast. The blood from the wretched man who had been killed had hardly dried in the square when a huge vat of beer was brought there, and pigs were roasted on spits so that the fumes lay thick over Wild Rose Valley, and all the Tengilmen ate and drank and boasted about Tengil, who gave them so many good things.

"But they're Wild Rose Valley's pigs they're eating, the bandits," said Mathias, "and Wild Rose Valley's beer they're drinking."

Tengil himself was not at the feast. When he had finished pointing, he had gone back across the river.

"And now he's probably sitting contentedly in his castle, thinking he's struck terror into Wild Rose Valley," said Jonathan, as we walked home. "He probably thinks that there is nothing left here but terrified bondsmen now."

"But he's wrong there," said Mathias. "What he doesn't understand, that Tengil, is that he can never subdue people who are fighting for their freedom and who stick together as we do."

We went past a little house with apple trees all around it, and Mathias said:

"That's where the man they killed lived."

A woman was sitting on the steps outside. I recognized her from the square and remembered how she had screamed when Tengil had pointed at her husband. Now she was sitting with a pair of scissors in her hand, and she was cutting off her long fair hair.

"What are you doing, Antonia?" Mathias said. "What are you going to do with your hair?"

"Bowstrings," she said.

She didn't say anything else, but I'll never forget the look in her eyes when she said that.

Many things brought the death penalty in Wild Rose Valley, Jonathan had told me, but the worst offense was to carry weapons; that was forbidden more than anything else. Tengil's soldiers went around looking everywhere in houses and yards, hunting for hidden bows and arrows and hidden swords and spears. But they never found anything. And yet there wasn't a house or a yard where there weren't weapons hidden and weapons forged for the battle that had to come in the end, Jonathan said.

Tengil had also promised white horses as a reward for those who revealed secret weapon hoards.

"How foolish," said Mathias. "Does he really think that there's a single traitor here in Wild Rose Valley?"

"No, it's only in Cherry Valley where there's one," said Jonathan sadly. Yes, I knew it was Jonathan walking there beside me, but it was difficult to remember it, the way he looked with that beard and those rags.

"Jossi hasn't seen what we've seen of cruelty and oppression," said Mathias. "Otherwise he could never do what he's doing."

"I wonder what Sofia's doing?" said Jonathan. "And I'd like to know if Bianca got there alive."

"We must hope that she did," said Mathias. "And that Sofia has put a stop to Jossi by now."

When we got back to Mathias's house, we saw Fatty Dodik lying in the grass, playing dice with three other Tengilmen. They must have been off duty, I think, because they lay there among the wild rose bushes all the afternoon. We could see them from the kitchen window. They played dice and ate meat and drank beer, which they had brought from the square, whole pails full. Gradually they gave up playing dice. Then they ate the meat and drank beer. Then they just drank beer. And then they did nothing, just crawled around like beetles in the bushes. Finally, they all four fell asleep.

Their helmets and cloaks lay in the grass where they had flung them, for no one could drink beer in a thick woolen cloak on such a warm day, could he?

"But if Tengil knew, he'd have them flogged," said Jonathan.

Then he vanished out through the door, and before I even had time to be afraid he was back with a cloak and a helmet.

"What do you want those dreadful things for?" said Mathias.

"I don't know yet," said Jonathan. "But a time may come when I'll need them."

"A time may come when you'll be caught, too," said Mathias.

But Jonathan tore off his beard and rags and put on the helmet and cloak, and there he stood, looking just like a Tengilman; it was horrible. Mathias shuddered and asked him for God's sake to hide the dreadful things in the hideout.

Jonathan did so.

Then we lay down and slept for the rest of the day, so I don't know what happened when Fatty Dodik and his companions woke up and started sorting out whose helmet and whose cloak had gone.

Mathias was asleep too, but he woke for a while, he told us afterward, to the sound of shouts and swearing from out in the wild rose thickets.

That night, we went on working on the underground passage.

"Three more nights," said Jonathan, "no more."

"And what's going to happen then?" I asked.

"Then what I've come for will happen," said Jonathan. "Maybe it won't be successful, but I must try anyhow. To free Orvar."

"Not without me," I said. "You can't leave me behind again. Wherever you go, I'm coming with you."

He looked at me for a long time, and then he smiled.

"Well, if you really want to, then that's what I want," he said.

CHAPTER ELEVEN

TENGIL'S SOLDIERS WERE ALL REVIVED BY SO much meat and beer, and every one of them must have wanted those twenty white horses, for they started frantically searching for Jonathan. They foraged about from morning to night, searching every house and every corner in the valley. Jonathan had to stay in his hideout until he was almost suffocated.

Veder and Kader rode around everywhere, reading out the proclamation about my brother. I, too, took the opportunity of hearing about "Tengil's enemy, Jonathan Lionheart, who had illegally surmounted the wall and whose whereabouts in Wild Rose Valley were still unknown." They described him, too: "A remarkably handsome youth, with fair hair, dark blue eyes, and slim of figure," they said, and that was how Jossi had described him, I'm sure. And again I heard about the death penalty for sheltering Lionheart and the reward for the person who betrayed him.

While Veder and Kader were riding around trumpeting all this, people were coming to Mathias's house to say farewell to Jonathan, and to thank him for everything he had done for them, which was probably a lot more than I knew about.

"We'll never forget you," they said with tears in their eyes, and they brought bread with them and gave it to him, although they had hardly anything to eat themselves.

"You'll need it, because it's a difficult and dangerous journey you're undertaking," they said, and then they hurried away to listen to Veder and Kader once again, just for the fun of it.

Soldiers came to Mathias's house too. I was sitting terrified on a chair in the kitchen as they came in, not daring to move, but Mathias was bold.

"What are you looking for?" he said. "I don't believe that Lionheart youth even exists. It's something you've invented so that you can go around messing up people's houses."

They certainly messed up the place. They began in the little bedroom, where they tipped all the bedclothes onto the floor. Then they rummaged through a cupboard in there, throwing out everything that was inside it, which was fairly silly. Did they really think Jonathan was hiding in a cupboard?

"Aren't you going to look inside the pot cupboard too?" asked Mathias. But that made them angry.

Then they came out into the kitchen and set about the sideboard, and I sat on my chair feeling the hatred riding up inside me. It was that evening that we were going to leave the valley, Jonathan and I, and I thought that if they found him now, I wouldn't know what I'd do. Things *couldn't* be so cruel that they caught Jonathan during his last hours in the valley.

Mathias had stuffed the sideboard full of old clothes, sheep's wool and things, to muffle any sound from the hideout, and they hauled the whole lot out on to the kitchen floor.

111

And then! Then I wanted to scream so that the house fell down; yes, because one of them put his shoulder against the sideboard to push it to one side. But no sound came out of me. I sat paralyzed on my chair and just hated him, everything about him, his rough hands and thick neck and that wart on his forehead. I hated him because I knew he was now going to see the shutter leading into the hideout, and that would be the end of Jonathan.

But a cry came from Mathias:

"Look! Fire!" he shouted. "Has Tengil ordered you to set fire to our houses too?"

I don't know how it had happened, but it was true. The sheep's wool on the floor was burning briskly, and the soldiers had to hurry to put it out. They jumped and stamped and cursed and swore, and finally they tipped the water-barrel over it all, so the fire was out almost before it had started. But Mathias grumbled all the same and was angry with them.

"Have you no sense at all?" he said. "You can't throw wool down like that right next to a fire, where there are flames and sparks!"

The soldier with the wart was furious.

"Shut up, old man!" he said. "Or I know several ways of shutting that mouth of yours."

But Mathias would not let them frighten him.

"I hope you're going to clean up after you," he said. "Just look what you've done! The place looks like a pigsty."

That was the right way to get them to go away.

"Clean up your own pigsty, old man," said the man with the wart, and he went out first, the others following, leaving the door wide open behind them.

"They've got no sense at all," said Mathias.

"What luck the fire started, though," I said. "What luck for Jonathan."

Mathias blew on his fingertips.

"Yes, small fires are quite good things sometimes," he said. "Though you get burned when you scrape red-hot charcoal out of the fire with your fingers."

But that wasn't the end of our miseries, whatever I'd thought. They searched the stable for Jonathan, too, and then the soldier with the wart came to Mathias and said:

"You've got two horses, old man! No one in Wild Rose Valley is allowed more than one, you know that. We'll send a man over from the other side tonight. He'll fetch the one with a white blaze; you'll have to give that one to Tengil."

"But it's the boy's horse," said Mathias.

"Oh, yes? But it's Tengil's now."

That's what that soldier said, and I began to cry. We had to leave Wild Rose Valley that evening, Jonathan and I. Our long underground passage was finished. Not until that moment had I even thought about it—how on earth were we going to take Grim and Fyalar with us? They couldn't crawl along an underground passage. What a fool I was not to have thought about that before, that we'd have to leave our horses with Mathias. That was bad enough, but why should things turn out even worse? Tengil would take Fyalar; I can't understand why my heart didn't break when I heard that.

The soldier with the wart hauled a little wooden tag out of his pocket and held it under Mathias's nose.

"Here," he said. "Write your house mark on this."

"Why should I do that?" said Mathias.

"That means it'll be a pleasure for you to give a horse to Tengil."

"I feel no such pleasure."

But then the soldier drew his sword.

"You certainly do," he said. "You feel great pleasure and

this is where you put your house mark. And then you give the tag to the man who comes over from Karmanyaka to fetch the horse, because Tengil wants proof that you've given it voluntarily, do you see, old man?" he said, pushing Mathias so that he almost fell over.

What else could Mathias do? He wrote down his house mark, and the soldiers went off to search elsewhere for Jonathan.

It was our last evening with Mathias. For the last time we sat down at his table, and for the last time he offered us soup. We were sad, all three of us, I most of all. I cried. Because of Fyalar. Because of Mathias. He had almost been my grandfather, and now I was going to leave him. I wept, too, because I was small and scared and could do nothing about soldiers coming like that and pushing my grandfather around.

Jonathan was sitting in silence, thinking, and suddenly he mumbled:

"If only I knew the password."

"What password?" I said.

"You have to say the password when you go in or out through the main gateway, didn't you know that?" he said.

"Yes, I know that," I said. "And I know what the password is, too. 'All power to Tengil, our liberator.' I heard Jossi say it. Didn't I tell you?"

Jonathan stared at me; for a long while he just stared at me, and then he began to laugh.

"Rusky, I do like you," he said. "Did you know that?"

I didn't understand why he was so pleased about the password, because he wasn't going through the gateway anyhow, but I was also a little pleased in all my misery because I had been able to cheer him up with such a small matter.

Mathias had gone into the bedroom to clear up and Jonathan

rushed in after him. They talked in low voices to each other in there, but I didn't hear much, except when Jonathan said:

"If I fail, then you'll look after my brother, won't you?"

Then he came back in to me.

"Listen now, Rusky," he said. "I'll take the pack and go on ahead, and you must wait here with Mathias, until you hear from me again. It'll take quite a while, because I've got a few things to arrange first."

Oh, how I disliked that. I've never been able to stand waiting for Jonathan, especially when I'm afraid all the time, and I was afraid now, for who knows what might happen to Jonathan on the other side of the wall, and what was he thinking of doing that might fail?

"You mustn't be so frightened," said Jonathan. "You're Karl Lionheart these days. Don't forget that."

Then he bade Mathias and me a hasty farewell, crawled into the hideout, and I saw him vanish down into the underground passage. He waved; the last thing I saw was his hand waving to us.

And then we were left alone, Mathias and I.

"Fatty Dodik doesn't know what kind of mole there is bur-rowing under his wall at this moment," said Mathias.

"No, but suppose he sees that mole sticking its head up through the earth," I said. "And then throws his spear!"

I was sad, and I crept out to the stable to Fyalar, for the last time seeking comfort from him. But he couldn't comfort me, for I knew that after this evening, I would never see him again.

It was dim in the stable, the window small, letting in very little light, but I saw how eagerly Fyalar turned his head as I came in through the door. I went over to the stall and threw my arms around his neck. I wanted him to understand that what had to happen wasn't my fault.

"Though perhaps it is my fault," I said, and I wept. "If I'd stayed in Cherry Valley, then Tengil would never have gotten hold of you. Forgive me, Fyalar, forgive me. But I couldn't do anything else."

I think he knew I was sad. He nuzzled my ear with his soft nose as if he didn't want me to cry.

But I cried. I stood there with him and I cried and cried, until there were no more tears inside me. Then I groomed him and gave him the last of the oats; well, he shared them with Grim, of course.

I thought such terrible thoughts as I groomed Fyalar.

May he drop dead, the man who was to come and fetch my horse, I thought. May he die before he gets across the river. It was terrible to wish things like that, it really was, and it didn't help, either.

No, he was almost certainly already on board the ferry, I thought, the ferry they carry all their stolen goods away on. Perhaps he had already landed? Perhaps he was just coming through the gateway and would be here any minute now? Oh, Fyalar, if only we could flee together, you and I.

Just as I was thinking like that, someone opened the stable door and I cried out, I was so frightened. But it was only Mathias. He had begun to wonder what I was doing. I was glad the light was dim in the stable, so that he couldn't see that I had been crying again. But he probably realized that I had, all the same, for he said:

"Little lad, if only I could do something. But no grandfather can help with this. So just cry."

Then I saw through the window behind him that someone was out there, coming toward Mathias's place. A Tengilman! The one who was coming to fetch Fyalar!

"He's coming!" I cried. "Mathias, he's coming!"

Fyalar whinnied, upset when I cried out so despairingly.

The next moment, the stable door was jerked open, and he was standing there in his black helmet and black cloak.

"No!" I cried. "No, no!"

But then he was already by me, and he threw his arms around me.

Jonathan did, for it was him!

"Don't you recognize your own brother?" he said as I struggled against him. He pulled me over to the window so that I could see him properly, and yet I could hardly believe it was Jonathan. He was unrecognizable. Because he was ugly. Uglier than me, even, and certainly not a "remarkably handsome youth." His hair was hanging down in wet strips and wasn't shining like gold, and he had stuffed a peculiar lump of snuff under his upper lip. I didn't know anyone could become so ugly with so little. He looked funny. I would have laughed if there had been time, but Jonathan clearly had no time for anything.

"Quick, quick!" he said. "I must leave at once. The man from Karmanyaka will be here any minute now."

He held out his hand toward Mathias.

"Give me the tag," he said. "For I'm sure you'll give both your horses to Tengil with great pleasure, won't you?"

"Yes, what do you think?" said Mathias, pressing the tag into his hand.

Jonathan put it into his pocket.

"I have to show that at the gateway," he said. "Then the Senior Guard will know I'm not lying."

It all happened so quickly. We saddled the horses faster than ever before, while Jonathan told us how he had got in through the great gateway, because Mathias wanted to know.

"It was simple," said Jonathan. "I gave the password that Rusky had taught me—'All power to Tengil, our liberator'—

and then the Senior Guard said: 'Where have you come from, where are you going, and what is your errand?' 'From Kar-manyaka to Mathias's Farm to fetch two horses for Tengil,' I said. 'Pass, then,' he said. 'Thank you,' I said. And here I am. But I must get back through the gate before the next Tengilman comes and wants to get in; otherwise things will be difficult."

We got the horses out of the stable faster than I can say, and Jonathan swung himself up into Grim's saddle, holding Fyalar by the reins beside him.

"Look after yourself, Mathias," he said. "Until we meet again."

Then he trotted away with the two horses, just like that.

"But what about me?" I shouted. "What shall I do?"

Jonathan waved to me.

"Mathias will tell you," he called.

And there I stood, staring after him, feeling stupid. But Mathias explained.

"You must see that *you* couldn't get through the gateway," he said. "You'll have to crawl along the passage as soon as it's dark. Then Jonathan will be on the other side waiting for you."

"Are you certain?" I said. "Something might happen to him at the last minute."

Mathias sighed.

"Nothing's certain in a world where there's Tengil," he said. "But if it goes wrong, then you'll have to come back and stay with me."

I tried to think what it would be like: first crawling along the passage all by myself—that alone was horrible—and then com-ing out into the forest on the other side of the wall, waiting and waiting, and at last realizing that it had all gone wrong. Then crawling back again, and living without Jonathan!

We were standing outside the now empty stable and sud-denly I thought of something else, too.

"What'll happen to you, Mathias, when he comes, that man from Karmanyaka, and there's no horse in the stable?"

"Yes, there'll be a horse, there," said Mathias. "Because I'm just off to fetch my own. I've been keeping it at the neighboring farm while Grim has been in my stable."

"But then he'll take your horse instead," I said.

"Just let him try!" said Mathias.

Mathias fetched his own horse back just in time, for soon afterward, the man who had come to fetch Fyalar did appear. At first he shouted and raged and scolded like all other Tengilmen because there was only one horse in the stable and because Mathias wouldn't hand it over.

"Don't try that one on me," said Mathias. "We're allowed *one* horse, you know that. And you've already taken away the other one and had my house mark for it. I can't help it if you've made a muddle of everything, so that one fathead doesn't know what the other one is doing."

Some Tengilmen became angry when Mathias turned haughty on them like that, but some became humble and meek. The man who had come to fetch Fyalar gave in at once.

"There must have been some mistake," he said and slouched off toward the path like a dog with its tail between its legs.

"Mathias, are you never afraid?" I asked when he was out of sight.

"Yes, of course, I'm afraid," said Mathias. "Feel my heart thumping," he went on, taking my hand and laying it on his chest. "We're all afraid," he said. "But sometimes you mustn't let it show."

Then the evening came, and darkness, so it was time for me to leave Wild Rose Valley and Mathias.

"Good-by, little lad," said Mathias. "Don't forget your grandfather."

"No, never," I said. "I'll never forget you!"

Then I was alone in the underground passage. I crawled along the long dark tunnel and I talked to myself all the way to keep myself calm and not to be too frightened.

"No, it doesn't matter at *all* that it's pitch dark . . . no, of *course* you won't suffocate . . . yes, a little earth *is* running down your neck, but that *doesn't* mean that the whole passage is going to collapse, you stupid thing! No, no, Dodik *can't* see you when you come up; he's not a cat that can see in the dark, is he? Yes, of *course* Jonathan's there waiting for you; he *is* there, do you hear what I'm saying? He *is*. He *is*!"

And he was. He was sitting there on a stone in the dark, and a little way away from him Grim and Fyalar were standing under a tree.

"Well, Karl Lionheart," he said. "Here you are at last."

CHAPTER TWELVE

WE SLEPT UNDER A FIR TREE THAT NIGHT AND woke at dawn; it was freezing cold, at least I was. Mist was lying between the trees and we could hardly see Grim and Fyalar. They looked like two gray ghost horses in the gray light and the silence all around us. It was utterly silent, dismal in some way. I don't know why everything seemed so gloomy and desolate and worrying that morning. All I know is that I longed to be back in Mathias's warm kitchen and I was uneasy about what lay ahead of us, everything that I knew nothing about.

I tried not to show Jonathan what I was feeling, for who knows, perhaps he would suggest that I go back, and I *wanted* to be with him through every danger, however great it was.

Jonathan looked at me and smiled slightly.

"Don't look like that, Rusky," he said. "This is nothing. Things'll get much worse, you can be sure."

Well, what a comfort *that* was! But just then the sun broke through, the mist vanished, the birds began to sing in the forest, all that had been gloomy and desolate disappeared, and the

121

dangers seemed less dangerous. I grew warm, too, and everything felt better, almost good.

Grim and Fyalar were also all right. They had got out of their dark stable and could now graze the rich green grass again. They liked that, I'm sure.

Jonathan whistled to them, a quiet little whistle, but they heard it and came.

He wanted to get away, now, Jonathan. Far away. At once!

"Because the wall's just behind that hazel thicket," he said. "And I've no desire to see the whites of Dodik's eyes."

Our underground passage came up between two nearby hazelnut bushes, but the opening could no longer be seen because Jonathan had covered it with branches and twigs. He marked the place with two sticks so that we would be able to find it again.

"Don't forget what it looks like," he said. "Remember that big stone and the fir tree where we slept, and the hazel thicket. Because one day we may come this way. If . . ."

He said no more and we mounted our horses and rode silently away.

Then a pigeon came flying over the treetops, one of Sofia's white pigeons.

"There's Paloma," said Jonathan, though I don't know how he could recognize her at such a distance.

We had waited a long time for news from Sofia, and now at last her pigeon had come, just when we were outside the wall. She flew straight toward Mathias's house and would soon be landing in the pigeon loft outside the stable. But only Mathias would be there to read her message.

This vexed Jonathan.

"If only she'd come yesterday," he said. "Then I'd have known what I want to know."

But we had to be away now, far away from Wild Rose Valley and the wall and all the Tengilmen searching for Jonathan.

We were to make our way down to the river via a detour through the forest, Jonathan said, and then follow the banks toward Karma Falls.

"And there, little Karl, you'll see a waterfall such as you've never even dreamt about."

I had seen very little before I had come to Nangiyala, certainly no forest like the one we were now riding through. It was one of those truly sagalike forests, thick and dark, and there were no trodden paths. We simply rode straight on through the trees, which slapped their wet branches across your face. But I liked it, all the same. All of it—seeing the sun sifting through the tree trunks, hearing the birds, and smelling the scent of trees and wet grass and horses. Most of all, I liked riding there with Jonathan.

The air was fresh and cool in the forest, but as we went on, it grew warmer. It was going to be a hot day, we could feel that already.

Soon Wild Rose Valley was left far behind us and we were deep in the forest. In a glade surrounded by tall trees, we came across a little gray cottage, right in the middle of the dark forest. How could anyone live in such a lonely place! But someone did live there, for smoke was coming out of the chimney and there were two goats grazing outside.

"Elfrida lives here," said Jonathan. "She'll give us a little goat's milk if we ask her."

We were given milk, as much as we liked, which was good, because we'd ridden a long way and had had nothing to eat. We sat on Elfrida's steps and drank her goat's milk, and we ate bread that we'd had with us and goat's cheese which Elfrida gave us, and we each had a fistful of wild strawberries which

I'd picked in the forest. It all tasted very good and we were satisfied.

Elfrida was a fat, kindly little old woman, and she lived alone there with nothing but her goats and a gray cat for company.

"Thank the Lord I don't live behind any walls," she said.

She knew many people in Wild Rose Valley and she wanted to know if they were still alive, so Jonathan had to tell her. He was sad when he did that, for most of it was the kind of news a kindly old person must grieve to hear.

"That things should be so wretched in Wild Rose Valley," Elfrida said. "A curse on Tengil! And on Katla! Everything would be all right, if only he hadn't got Katla."

She threw her apron over her eyes, and I think she was crying.

I couldn't bear to watch, so I went to find some more wild strawberries: who was Katla and where was Katla? When would I be told that?

We got to the river in the end, in the heat of the midday sun. The sun was sitting like a ball of fire in the sky and the water glittered too, flashing like a thousand little suns. We stood high up on the steep bank and saw the river far below us. What a sight it was! The river of The Ancient Rivers was rushing toward Karma Falls so that the foam swirled. It wanted to get there with all those mighty waters, and we could hear the falls thundering in the distance.

We wanted to go down to the water to cool off. Grim and Fyalar were let loose in the forest to find themselves a stream to drink from, but we wanted to bathe in the river. So we rushed down the steep slope, almost tearing our clothes off as we ran. There were willow trees down on the riverbank, and one of them had grown right out over the river, dragging its branches in the water. We climbed along the trunk and Jonathan showed me how I should hold on to a branch and let myself down into the swirling water.

"But don't let go," he said, "or you'll get to Karma Falls far quicker than is good for you."

I held on so hard that my knuckles turned white. I swung there on my branch and let the water rush over me; never have I had such a wonderful bath, nor such a dangerous one. I felt the pull of Karma Falls right through my body.

Then I climbed up onto the trunk again, Jonathan helping me, and we sat in the crown of the willow as if in a green house swaying over the water. The river leapt and played directly below us, trying to lure us in again, trying to make us think it wasn't at all dangerous. But I only needed to dip my toes in, and in my big toe alone I could feel that pull that wanted to take me with it.

As I was sitting there, I happened to look up the slope and then I grew frightened. There were riders up there, Tengil soldiers with long spears. They were coming at a gallop, but we hadn't heard the sound of their hoofs because of the roar of the water.

Jonathan saw them too, but I could see no sign that he was afraid. We sat there silently, waiting for them to ride past. But they didn't ride past. They stopped and jumped down from their horses as if they were going to take a rest or something like that.

I asked Jonathan:

"Is it you they're after, do you think?"

"No," said Jonathan. "They come from Karmanyaka and are on their way to Wild Rose Valley. There's a suspension bridge over the river at Karma Falls. Tengil usually sends his soldiers that way."

"But they needn't have stopped just here," I said.

Jonathan agreed with me.

"I really don't want them to see me," he said, "and get funny ideas about Lionhearts into their heads."

I counted six of them up there on the slope. They were talking and arguing about something, pointing down towards the water, though we couldn't hear what they were saying. But suddenly one of them started riding his horse down the slope toward the river. He came riding almost straight at us, and I was glad we were sitting so well hidden in the tree.

The others shouted after him:

"Don't do it, Park! You'll drown yourself and your horse!"

But he—the one they called Park—just laughed and shouted back:

"I'll show you! If I don't get to that rock and back, then I'll stand you all a beer, I swear!"

Then we realized what he was going to do.

There was a rock protruding out of the river some way out. The currents were swirling around it and only a little of it showed above the surface. But Park must have happened to see it as he was riding past, and now he was showing off.

"The fool," said Jonathan. "Does he think a horse can swim against the current all the way out there!"

Park had already flung off his helmet and cloak and boots, and in nothing but his shirt and trousers he was trying to force the horse down into the river. A lovely little black mare it was. Park shouted and swore and urged, but the mare was unwilling. She was afraid. Then he hit her. He had no riding crop but hit her on the head with his fists, and I heard Jonathan draw in a deep breath like a sob, just as he had done that time in the square.

At last Park had his own way; the mare neighed, and terrified, she hurled herself into the river just because that madman wanted her to. It was terrible to see how she struggled when the current caught her.

"She'll drift right down toward us," said Jonathan. "Park can do as he likes, but he'll never get her to that rock."

But she tried, she really tried. Oh, how she struggled and what terror she felt when she sensed that the river was stronger than she was!

Even Park eventually realized that his life was now at stake, and then he tried to get her back to the bank, but he soon saw that she couldn't manage. No, because the currents wished otherwise; they wished to take him to Karma Falls, a fate he thoroughly deserved. But the mare, I felt sorry for her. She was quite helpless now, and they came drifting toward us just as Jonathan had said; soon they would pass us and disappear. I could see the terror in Park's eyes; no doubt he knew what was going to happen.

I turned my head to see where Jonathan was and cried out when I saw him. He was hanging from the branch, dangling over the water as far out as he could get, upside down, his legs hooked around the branch, and just as Park came immediately below him, Jonathan grabbed him by the hair and pulled him in so that he could catch hold of a branch.

And then Jonathan called to the mare.

"Come, little mare, come here!"

She had already drifted past, but she made a wild attempt to get back to him. She didn't have that great lump Park on her back now, but she was almost sinking. Then in some way Jonathan got hold of her reins and began to tug and pull at them. It grew into a tug-of-war between life and death, for the river did not wish to let go; it wanted both the mare and Jonathan.

I grew quite wild and shouted at Park:

"Help them, you big ox, you! Help them!"

He had scrambled up into the tree and was sitting there safe and sound, quite near Jonathan, but the only thing the fool did to help was to lean forward and yell:

"Let the horse go! There are two horses up there in the forest. I can take one of those instead. Just let it go!"

You grow strong when you're angry, I've always heard, and in that way you could say that Park helped Jonathan save the mare.

But afterward he said to Park:

"You blockhead, you, do you think I'd save your life so that you could steal my horse? Aren't you ashamed of yourself?"

Perhaps Park was ashamed, I don't know. He said nothing and he never even asked who we were or anything. He just clambered up the slope with his poor mare, and soon afterward he and the whole troop disappeared.

We made a campfire above Karma Falls that evening, and I'm sure no campfire in any day or in any world has burned on a campsite like the one where we lit ours.

It was a dreadful place, terrible and beautiful, like no other place in heaven or on earth, I think: the mountains and the river and the waterfall, it was all too vast, all of it. Again, I felt as if I were in a dream, and I said to Jonathan:

"This can't be real. It's like something out of an ancient dream."

We were standing on the bridge then, the bridge that Tengil had had built over the chasm separating the two countries, Karmanyaka and Nangiyala, on either side of the river of The Ancient Rivers.

The river was rushing along deep down in the depths below the bridge, then throwing itself with a great roar over Karma Falls, an even deeper and more terrible chasm.

I asked Jonathan:

"How do you build a bridge over such a terrible chasm?"

"I'd like to know that, too," he said. "And how many human lives went into building it? How many people fell down there with a cry and vanished into Karma Falls? I'd like to know that very much."

I shuddered, thinking I could hear the cries still echoing between the mountain walls.

We were very near Tengil's country now. On the other side of the bridge, I could see a path winding its way up through the mountains: The Ancient Mountains of Karmanyaka.

"If you follow that path, you come to Tengil's castle," said Jonathan.

I shuddered again, but I thought things could do what they liked tomorrow—this evening, I was going to sit by a campfire with Jonathan for the first time in my life.

We had our fire on a ledge of rock high up above the waterfall, near the bridge. But I sat with my back to everything, because I didn't want to see the bridge over to Tengil's country or anything else, either. I saw only the light from the fire flickering between the mountain walls, and that was beautiful and a little terrible, too. And then I saw Jonathan's handsome, kindly face in the firelight, and the horses, which were standing resting a little way away.

"This is much better than my last campfire," I said. "Because now I'm here with you, Jonathan."

Wherever I was, I felt safe as long as Jonathan was with me, and I was happy that at last I could sit by a campfire with him, what he had talked about so many times when we had lived on earth.

"The days of campfires and sagas, do you remember saying that?" I said to Jonathan.

"Yes, I remember," said Jonathan. "But then I didn't know there were such evil sagas here in Nangiyala."

"Must it always be like this?" I asked.

129

He sat in silence for a while, staring into the fire, and then he said:

"No. When the final battle is over, then Nangiyala will probably again be a country where the sagas are beautiful and life will be easy and simple to live, as before."

The fire flared up, and in the light, I saw how tired and sad he was.

"But the final battle, you see, Rusky, can only be an evil saga of death and death and more death. So Orvar must lead that battle, not me. For I'm no good at killing."

No, I know that, I thought. And then I asked him:

"Why did you save that man Park's life? Was that a good thing?"

"I don't know whether it was a good thing," said Jonathan. "But there are things you *have* to do, otherwise you're not a human being but just a bit of filth. I've told you that before."

"But suppose he'd realized who you were?" I said. "And they'd caught you?"

"Well, then they would have caught Lionheart and not a bit of filth," said Jonathan.

Our fire burned down and the darkness sank over the mountains, first a brief dusk for a moment turning everything almost mild and friendly and soft, then a black, roaring darkness, in which you could hear nothing but Karma Falls and see no glimmer of light anywhere.

I crept as close to Jonathan as I could, and we sat there, leaning against the mountain wall, talking to each other in the dark. I wasn't afraid, but a strange unease had come over me. We ought to sleep, Jonathan said, but I knew that I couldn't sleep. I could hardly speak either, because of that feeling of anxiety, which had nothing to do with the dark, but something else, I didn't know what. And yet Jonathan was there beside me.

130

There was a flash of lightning and then a crash of thunder, the sound booming against the mountain walls, and then it came over us, a storm beyond all imagination, the thunder rolling over the mountains with a roar that drowned even the sound of Karma Falls, and flashes of lightning coming one after another. Sometimes the light flared up and the next moment it was darker than ever; it was as if a night from ancient times had fallen over us.

And then there was another flash of lightning, more terrible than any of the others, flaring up and throwing its light over everything.

And then, in that light, I saw Katla. *I saw Katla.*

CHAPTER THIRTEEN

YES, I SAW KATLA, BUT I DON'T KNOW WHAT happened next. I just sank into the black depths and didn't wake up until the thunderstorm had passed and light was already beginning to appear behind the mountain peaks. I was lying with my head in Jonathan's lap, and terror washed over me as soon as I remembered—there, far away on the other side of the river, was where Katla had stood on a cliff, high up above Karma Falls. I whimpered when I recalled it, and Jonathan tried to comfort me.

"She isn't there any longer. She's gone now."

But I wept and asked him:

"How can things like Katla exist? Is it—a monster, or what?"

"Yes, she's a monster," said Jonathan. "A female dragon risen from ancient times, that's what she is, and she's as cruel as Tengil himself."

"Where did he get her from?" I asked.

"She came out of Katla Cavern—that's what people think," said Jonathan. "She fell asleep down there one night in ancient

132

times and slept for thousands upon thousands of years, and no one knew she existed. But one morning, she woke up; one terrible morning, she came crawling into Tengil's castle, spurting death-dealing fire at everyone, and they fell in all directions in her path."

"Why didn't she kill Tengil?" I said.

"Tengil fled for his life through the great rooms of his castle. As she approached him, he tore down a great battlehorn used for calling up soldiers to help, and when he blew the horn . . ."

"What happened then?" I asked.

"Then Katla came crawling to him like a dog. Ever since that day, she has obeyed Tengil. And Tengil alone. She's afraid of his battlehorn. When he blows it, she obeys blindly."

It was getting lighter and lighter. The mountain peaks over in Karmanyaka were glowing like Katla's fire, and we were going to Karmanyaka now! How frightened I was, oh, how terribly afraid! Who knew where Katla was lying in wait? Where was she, where did she live, did she live in Katla Cavern, and how could Orvar then be there? I asked Jonathan and he told me how things were.

Katla didn't live in Katla Cavern. She had never gone back there after her long and ancient sleep; no, Tengil kept her tethered in a cave near Karma Falls. In that cave she was chained with a chain of gold, Jonathan said, and there she had to stay, except when Tengil took her with him to instill terror into people he wished to terrorize.

"I saw her in Wild Rose Valley once," said Jonathan.

"And did you cry out?" I said.

"Yes, I cried out," he said.

The terror grew in me.

"I'm so afraid, Jonathan. Katla will kill us."

He tried to calm me again.

"But she is tethered. She can move no farther than the length of her chain, no farther than that cliff where you saw her. She stands there nearly all the time and stares down into Karma Falls."

"Why does she do that?" I said.

"I don't know," said Jonathan. "Perhaps she's looking for Karm."

"Who is Karm?" I asked.

"Oh, that's just Elfrida's talk," said Jonathan. "No one has ever seen Karm. He doesn't exist. But Elfrida says that once in ancient times he lived in Karma Falls and that Katla hated him then and cannot forget it. That's why she stands there staring."

"Who was he that he could live in such a terrible waterfall?" I said.

"He was a monster too," said Jonathan. "A sea serpent as long as the river is wide, Elfrida says. But that's probably only one of those old sagas."

"Perhaps he's no more a saga than Katla?" I said.

He didn't reply to that, but said:

"Do you know what Elfrida told me while you were in the forest picking wild strawberries? She said that when she was small, they used to frighten children with Karm and Katla. The saga of the dragon in Katla Cavern and the sea serpent in Karma Falls she'd heard many a time in her childhood, and she liked it very much just because it was so terrible. It was one of those ancient sagas that people have frightened children with in all times, Elfrida said."

"Couldn't Katla have stayed in her cavern, then," I said, "and gone on being a saga?"

"Yes, that's just what Elfrida thought, too," said Jonathan.

I shivered and wondered if Karmanyaka was a country full of monsters; I didn't want to go there. But I had to now.

We fortified ourselves from the food sack first, saving some food for Orvar because Jonathan said that starvation reigned in Katla Cavern.

Grim and Fyalar drank the rainwater that had collected in the crevices. There was no good grazing for them up here in the mountains, but a little grass was growing by the bridge, so I think they had had just about enough when we set off.

We rode across the bridge toward Karmanyaka, the country of Tengil, and the country of monsters. I was so frightened that I was shaking all over. That sea-serpent—perhaps I didn't seriously believe that he existed, but all the same, suppose he suddenly flung himself up out of the depths and pulled us down off the bridge to perish in Karma Falls? And then Katla; I dreaded her more than anything. Perhaps she was waiting for us now, over there on Tengil's shore, with her cruel fangs and her death-dealing fire. Oh, how frightened I was.

But we crossed the bridge, and I saw no Katla. She wasn't on her cliff, and I said to Jonathan:

"No, she isn't there."

And yet she was there. Not on the cliff, but her terrible head was protruding from behind a huge block of rock by the path up toward Tengil's castle. We saw her there. She saw us and let out a scream that could demolish mountains, jets of fire and smoke pouring out of her nostrils as she snorted with rage and jerked at her chain, jerking and jerking and screaming over and over again.

Grim and Fyalar were so beside themselves with terror that we could hardly hold them, and my terror was no less. I begged Jonathan to turn back to Nangiyala, but he said:

"We can't let Orvar down. Don't be afraid. Katla can't reach us, however much she drags and pulls at her chain."

And yet we had to hurry, he said, because Katla's screams

were a signal that could be heard as far up as Tengil's castle, and soon we would have a swarm of Tengil's soldiers on us if we didn't flee and hide in the mountains.

We rode on. We rode along wretched, narrow, steep mountain paths, riding so that sparks flew from us, riding hither and thither among the rocks to lead any pursuers astray. Every moment I expected to hear galloping horses behind us and shouts from Tengil's soldiers trying to get us with their spears and arrows and swords. But none came. It was probably difficult to follow anyone among Karmanyaka's many cliffs and mountains, where it was easy for the hunted to evade his pursuers.

When we had ridden for a long time, I asked Jonathan:

"Where are we going?"

"To Katla Cavern, of course," he said. "We're almost there now. That's Katla Mountain straight in front of you."

Yes, it was. In front of us was a low, flat mountain with steep slopes dropping straight downward. Only in our direction were they less steep and there we would easily be able to make our way up if we wanted to, which we did, for we had to get right across the mountain, Jonathan said.

"The entrance lies on the other side, toward the river," he said. "And I must see what happens there."

"Jonathan, do you really think we can ever get into Katla Cavern?" I said.

He had told me about the huge copper gate across the entrance to the cave, and about the Tengilmen who stood on guard outside day and night. How on earth were we going to get in?

He didn't answer me, but said that we would have to hide the horses now, for they couldn't climb mountains.

We led them into a sheltered crevice immediately below Katla Mountain and left them there, horses, packs, and everything. Jonathan patted Grim and said:

"Wait there. We're only going on a scouting trip."

I didn't like the idea because I didn't want to be separated from Fyalar, but that couldn't be helped.

It took us quite a time to get up on the mountain plateau, and I was tired when we eventually reached it. Jonathan said we could rest for a while, so I at once threw myself full length down on the ground. Jonathan did too, and we lay there, up on Katla mountain, the wide sky above us and Katla Cavern directly beneath us. It was strange to think about: inside the mountain somewhere beneath us was that terrible cavern with all its passages and caves, where so many people had languished and died. And out here butterflies were fluttering about in the sunlight, the sky above was blue with small white clouds, and flowers and grass were growing all around. It was strange that flowers and grass grew on the roof of Katla Cavern.

I wondered, if so many people had died in Katla Cavern, whether perhaps Orvar were also dead, and I asked Jonathan whether he thought so too. But he didn't reply. He just lay there staring straight up at the sky, thinking about something, I could see. Finally he said:

"If it's true that Katla slept her ancient sleep in Katla Cavern, then how did she get out when she awoke? The copper gate was already there then. Tengil has always used Katla Cavern as his prison."

"While Katla was sleeping inside?" I said.

"Yes, while Katla was sleeping inside," said Jonathan. "Without anyone's knowing about it."

I shivered. I couldn't imagine anything worse; think of sitting imprisoned in Katla Cavern and seeing a dragon come crawling along just like that!

But Jonathan had other thoughts in his head.

"She must have come out another way," he said. "And I *must* find that way even if it takes a year."

137

We couldn't stay any longer because Jonathan was so restless. We were heading for Katla Cavern, which was only a short walk across the mountain. We could already see the river far below us and Nangiyala over on the other side. Oh, how I longed to be there.

"Look, Jonathan," I said. "I can see the willow where we bathed. There, on the other side of the river."

But Jonathan made a sign for me to be quiet, afraid that someone might hear us because we were so close now. This was where Katla Mountain ended in a perpendicular cliff, and in the mountainside below us was the copper gate into Katla Cavern, Jonathan said, although we couldn't see it from up there.

But we could see the soldiers on guard, three Tengilmen; I only had to see their black helmets for my heart to begin thumping.

We had wriggled on our stomachs right to the edge of the precipice, to be able to look down at them; if only they had looked up, they would have seen us. But they could not have been more useless as guards, for they did not look in any direction, but just sat there playing dice, not bothering about anything else. No enemy could penetrate beyond the copper gate, so why should they keep watch?

Just then, we saw the gate swing open down there, and someone came out of the cave—another Tengilman. He was carrying an empty food bowl which he flung to the ground. The gate fell back behind him, and we could hear him locking it.

"Well, now that pig has been fed for the last time," he said.

The others laughed and one of them said:

"Did you tell him what a remarkable day it is today—the last day of his life? I suppose you told him that Katla is expecting him this evening when darkness falls?"

"Yes, and do you know what he said? 'Oh, yes. At last,' he said. And then he asked to be allowed to send a message to Wild Rose Valley. How did it go, now? 'Orvar may die, but freedom never!' "

"Ha!" said the other man. "He can tell that to Katla this evening and hear what she has to say."

I looked at Jonathan, who had turned pale.

"Come on," he said. "We must get away from here."

We crept away from the precipice as quickly and quietly as we could, and when we knew we were out of sight, we ran. All the way back, we ran without stopping until we got back to Grim and Fyalar.

We sat in the crevice with the horses because now we didn't know what to do. Jonathan was so sad and I could do nothing to comfort him, only be sad too. I realized how much he was grieving for Orvar. He had thought he would be able to help him, and now he no longer believed it.

"Orvar, my friend, whom I never met," he said. "Tonight you will die and what will then happen to Nangiyala's green valleys?"

We ate a little bread, which we shared with Grim and Fyalar. I would have liked a gulp or two of goat's milk too, because we had saved some.

"Not yet, Rusky," said Jonathan. "Tonight, when darkness has fallen, I'll give you every drop. But not before."

For a long while he sat there quite still and dispirited, but in the end he said:

"It'll be like looking for a needle in a haystack, I know. But we must try, all the same."

"Try what?" I said.

"To find out where Katla got out," he said.

Though I could see he didn't really believe in it himself.

"If we had a year," he said. "Then we might. But we've got only a day."

Just as he was saying it, something happened. In the narrow crevice where we were sitting, a few bushes were growing at the far end by the mountain wall, and out of those bushes a terrified fox suddenly appeared, slunk past us, and was gone almost before we had time to see him.

"Where on earth did that fox come from?" said Jonathan. "I must find out."

He vanished behind the bushes. I stayed where I was, waiting, but he was so long and so quiet, I grew uneasy in the end.

"Where are you, Jonathan?" I cried.

And then I really got an answer. He sounded quite wild.

"Do you know where that fox came from? From inside the mountain! Do you see, Rusky, from inside Katla Mountain! There's a big cave in there."

Perhaps everything had already been decided in the ancient days of the sagas. Perhaps Jonathan had been named as Orvar's savior even then, for the sake of Wild Rose Valley. And perhaps there were some secret saga-beings who guided our footsteps without our knowing it. Otherwise how could Jonathan have found a way into Katla Cavern precisely where we had happened to put our horses? It was just as strange as when among all the houses in Wild Rose Valley, I happened to find Mathias's and none other.

Katla's exit from Katla Cavern; that must be what Jonathan had found; we could not believe otherwise. It was a passage straight into the mountainside, not at all large, but large enough for a starving female dragon to make her way along, said Jonathan, if she had awakened after thousands of years and found her usual path closed by a copper gate.

And large enough for us. I stared into the dark hole. How

many sleeping dragons would there be in there, who would wake if you went in and happened to step on them? That was what I wondered.

Then I felt Jonathan's arm around my shoulders.

"Rusky," he said. "I don't know what's waiting in there in the dark, but I'm going in there now."

"So am I," I said, my voice trembling a little.

Jonathan stroked my cheek with his forefinger, as he used to do sometimes.

"Are you sure you wouldn't prefer to wait here with the horses?"

"Haven't I told you that wherever you go, I go, too?" I said.

"Yes, you told me that," said Jonathan, and he sounded quite glad.

"Because I want to be with you," I said. "Even if it's in an underground hell."

Katla Cavern was an underground hell. Creeping along that black hole was like creeping through an evil, black dream which you cannot wake up from; like going from sunlight into eternal night.

The whole of Katla Cavern was nothing but a dead old dragon's nest, I thought, reeking of wickedness from ancient times. No doubt thousands of dragon's eggs had been hatched out there, and cruel dragons had crawled out in hordes to kill everything in their way.

An old dragon's nest was just the kind of place Tengil would think of as suitable for a prison. I shivered when I thought of everything he had done to people in here. The air seemed to me to be thick with old dried wickedness, whisperings from far away inside the cave, which seemed to be about all the torment and tears and death which Katla Cavern had experienced during Tengil's reign. I wanted to ask Jonathan if he could hear the whisperings too, but I didn't, because I was probably imagining them.

"Now, Rusky, we're going on a walk that you'll never forget," said Jonathan.

It was true. We had to get right through the mountain to reach the prison cave where Orvar was just inside the copper gate. It was that cave that people meant when they spoke of Katla Cavern, Jonathan said, because they didn't know of any other cave. We didn't even really know whether it would be possible to reach underground. But we knew that the way there was going to be a long one, for we had walked that stretch before up on the mountain, and it would be seven times worse making our way down here through dark rambling passages, with only the light from the torches we had with us.

Oh, how terrible it was to see the torchlight flickering over the cave walls, only lighting up a little of the great darkness around us, and so everything outside the light seemed even more dangerous. Who knows, I thought, perhaps there were dragons and serpents and monsters galore lying in wait for us in their dark caves. I was also frightened that we would lose our way in the passages, but Jonathan made black soot marks with his torch as we went on so that we could find our way back.

Walk, Jonathan had said, but we didn't do much walking. We crept and crawled and climbed and swam and jumped and clambered and struggled and toiled and fell, that's what we did. What a walk! And what caves! Sometimes we came to huge caverns so vast that we could see no end to them, except for the echo which told us what huge rooms they were. Sometimes we had to go through places where you couldn't even stand up but had to crawl on your stomach like any other dragon. Sometimes the way was barred by underground streams which we had to swim across. And worst of all, sometimes great gaping chasms appeared at our feet. I nearly fell into one of these. I

142

was carrying the torch and I tripped, dropping the torch. We saw it falling like a stream of fire, farther and farther and farther down, until at last it disappeared, and we were left in the dark, the worst and darkest darkness in the world. I dared not move or talk or even think. I tried to forget that I existed, standing there in the black darkness on the edge of a chasm. But I heard Jonathan's voice beside me. He lit the other torch we had with us, meanwhile talking to me, talking and talking quite calmly, so that I wouldn't go mad with terror, I suppose.

So we toiled on, for how long I don't know, for in the depths of Katla Cavern there was no time. It seemed as if we had been wandering around for an eternity, and I began to fear that we wouldn't get there until it was too late. Perhaps it was too late already, perhaps darkness had already fallen out there, and Orvar . . . perhaps he was with Katla now?

I asked Jonathan if he thought so too.

"I don't know," he said. "But don't think about it now if you don't want to go mad."

We had come to a narrow, twisting path, which never seemed to come to an end, but simply grew narrower and more confined, bit by bit, shrinking in height and width until we could hardly go on, and finally it became just a hole into which you had to crawl to get through.

But on the other side of the hole we were suddenly in a large cavern, how large we couldn't tell, for the light from the torch did not reach very far. But Jonathan tested the echo.

"Ho-ho-ho," he called, and we heard the echo replying "ho-ho-ho" many times in many different directions.

But then we heard something else, another voice far away in the dark.

"Ho-ho-ho," it mocked. "What do you want, you who come in such strange ways with torches and light?"

"I'm looking for Orvar," said Jonathan.

"Orvar is here," said the voice. "And who are you?"

"I am Jonathan Lionheart," said Jonathan. "And with me is my brother, Karl Lionheart. We've come to save you, Orvar."

"Too late," said the voice. "Too late, but thanks all the same."

Hardly had the words been uttered when we heard the copper gate opening with a screech. Jonathan threw down his torch and stamped on it so that it went out; then we stood still and waited.

Through the gateway came a Tengilman with a lantern in his hand. I began to cry silently to myself, not because I was afraid, but for Orvar's sake. How could things be so cruel that they were coming to take him away at this very moment!

"Orvar from Wild Rose Valley, prepare yourself," said the Tengilman. "In a moment you'll be taken to Katla. The black escorts are on their way."

In the light of the lantern, we could see a large wooden cage made of rough timbers, and we realized that inside that cage, Orvar was imprisoned like an animal.

The Tengilman put the lantern down on the ground by the cage.

"You may have a lantern for your last hour. In his mercy, Tengil has decided that, so that you will get used to the light again and be able to see Katla when you meet her, which I'm sure you want to."

He cackled with laughter and then vanished through the gate, which fell back behind him with a crash.

By then we were already up to the cage and Orvar, and we could see him in the light of the lantern, a wretched sight, as he could hardly move, but he crawled up to the bars and stretched out his hands toward us through the timbers.

"Jonathan Lionheart," he said. "I've heard a lot about you

144

at home in Wild Rose Valley. And now you've come here."

"Yes, now I've come here," said Jonathan, and then I heard that he too was crying a little because of Orvar and his wretchedness. But then he whipped out the knife he kept in his belt and began hacking at the cage.

"Come on, Rusky! Help, now," he said, and I hacked with my knife too, though what could we do with two knives? What we needed was an ax and a saw.

But we hacked away with our knives until our hands were bleeding. We hacked and wept, for we knew we had come too late. Orvar knew it too, but perhaps he wished to believe that it wasn't true, for he was panting with excitement inside his cage, mumbling now and again:

"Hurry! Hurry!"

We hurried so that the blood ran. We hacked away wildly, every moment expecting the gate to open and the black escorts to come in. Then the end would have come for Orvar and for us and for the whole of Wild Rose Valley.

They won't be fetching only one, I thought. Katla will have three tonight.

I felt that I couldn't endure much more; my hands were shaking so that I could hardly hold the knife, and Jonathan was shouting with rage, rage against those timbers that would not give way, however much we hacked at them. He kicked them, shouted and kicked and hacked again and kicked again, and then at last there was a crash—at last one timber gave way. And then another. It was enough.

"Now, Orvar, now!" said Jonathan, but there was nothing but a gasp in reply. So Jonathan crawled into the cage and pulled out Orvar, who could neither stand nor walk. Neither could I, almost, by then, but I reeled ahead of them with the lantern, and Jonathan began to drag Orvar away toward our rescue hole. He was tired now and panting, too; yes, we were panting like hunted animals, all three of us, which was exactly what we felt like, too; at least I did.

However he managed it, Jonathan succeeded in dragging Orvar right across the cavern, squeezing into the hole and in some amazing way taking Orvar with him, now more dead than alive, as I felt then, too. Now it was my turn to creep through the hole, but I didn't get that far, for then we heard the screech of the gate and it was as if all the energy ran out of me and I couldn't move at all.

"Quick, quick, the lantern!" gasped Jonathan, and I handed it to him, although my hands were shaking. The lantern had to be hidden; the slightest glimmer would betray us.

The black escorts—they were already in the cavern, and more Tengilmen with lanterns in their hands. It grew terrifyingly light, but over in our corner it was dark and Jonathan bent down and grabbed my arms and pulled me through the hole into that dark passage behind, and there we lay, all three of us panting, listening to their cries.

"He's gone! He's gone!"

CHAPTER FOURTEEN

*T*HAT NIGHT WE CARRIED ORVAR THROUGH
hell. Jonathan did. He dragged Orvar through hell; there
was no other way of describing it. I only managed to drag myself, and only just that.

"He's gone! He's gone!" they had cried, and when silence
fell, we expected them to pursue us, but they didn't. Yet even
Tengilmen must have been able to reckon that there was a way
out of Katla Cavern through which we had gone, and that
wouldn't have been all that difficult to find. But they were
cowardly, the Tengilmen, daring to face the enemy when in a
herd, but not daring to be the first to crawl into a narrow
passageway where an unknown enemy was lying in wait. No,
they must have been too cowardly, for otherwise why had they
let us get away so easily? No one had ever escaped from Katla
Cavern before, and how would they explain Orvar's flight to
Tengil, I wondered? But that was their problem; we had quite
enough of our own.

147

Not until we had dragged ourselves through the long narrow passageway did we dare stop for a while to get our breath back, which we had to for Orvar's sake. Jonathan gave him goat's milk, which was sour, and bread, which was wet, but even so, Orvar said:

"I've never had a better meal."

Jonathan rubbed Orvar's long legs to bring some life back into them and he began to revive, though he couldn't walk, only crawl.

Jonathan told him which way we had to go, and asked him if he still wanted to go on that night.

"Yes, yes, yes," said Orvar. "I'll crawl all the way home to Wild Rose Valley if necessary. I don't want to lie here waiting for Tengil's bloodhounds to come howling along the passageways after us."

It was already noticeable who he was; no subdued prisoner, but a rebel and freedom fighter, Orvar of Wild Rose Valley. When I saw his eyes in the light of the lantern, I understood why Tengil was afraid of him. Weak though he was now, he had a kind of burning fire inside him, and it was probably that fire which carried him through that night of hell, for of all the nights in the whole world, none could have been worse.

It seemed an eternity, full of terrors, but when you're sufficiently exhausted, you don't worry about anything, not even whether there are bloodhounds after you; yes, we did hear the hounds coming, howling and baying, but I hadn't the *energy* to be afraid. Anyhow, they soon fell silent, for not even bloodhounds dared penetrate far into the depths where we were crawling.

We crawled along for a long, long time, and when we eventually came out into the daylight by Grim and Fyalar, battered and sore, blood-stained and soaked to the skin, almost dead with exhaustion, the night was over and the morning already there. Orvar stretched out his arms as if embracing the earth and the sky and everything he could see, but then his arms fell and he was asleep. We sank into a coma, all three of us, and we were unconscious until it was almost evening. Then I awoke. It was Fyalar nudging me with his nose. He no doubt thought I had slept long enough.

Jonathan was also awake.

"We must get out of Karmanyaka before dark," he said. "After dark, we won't be able to find the way."

He woke Orvar, and when Orvar came to life and sat up and looked around and realized that he was no longer in Katla Cavern, tears came into his eyes.

"Free," he mumbled. "Free."

He took Jonathan's hands and held them in his for a long time.

"My life and my freedom—you've given them back to me," he said, and he thanked me too, although I had done nothing and had mostly been in the way.

Orvar must have felt much as I had when I was released from all pain and had come to Cherry Valley. I longed for him to reach *his* valley alive and free, but we weren't there yet. We were still in the mountains of Karmanyaka, now probably seething with Tengil's soldiers searching for him. It was fortunate enough that they hadn't found us sleeping in our crevice.

We sat there eating the last of our bread, and after a while Orvar said:

"Just think, I'm alive! I'm alive and free!"

For he alone of the prisoners in Katla Cavern was alive; all the others had been sacrificed one by one to Katla.

"But you can trust Tengil," said Orvar. "Believe me, he'll see to it that Katla Cavern isn't empty for long."

Again tears came into his eyes.

"Oh, Wild Rose Valley of mine," he said, "how much longer will you have to sigh under Tengil?"

He wanted to know everything that had happened in the valleys of Nangiyala during his imprisonment; about Sofia and Mathias and everything Jonathan had done. Jonathan told him about Jossi too. I thought Orvar would die then, right in front of our eyes, when he heard that he had suffered for so long in Katla Cavern because of Jossi. There was a long pause before he pulled himself together and could speak again, and then he said:

"My life means nothing. But what Jossi has done to Wild Rose Valley can never be expiated or forgiven."

"Forgiven or not, he's probably been punished by now," said Jonathan. "I don't think you'll ever see Jossi again."

But rage had fallen over Orvar. He wanted to leave; it was almost as if he wished to start the struggle for freedom that very evening, and he swore at his legs because they carried him so badly, though he tried and tried and at last succeeded in getting up on them. He was quite proud when he was able to show us that, and he was certainly a sight as he stood there, swaying backward and forward as if he might be blown over any moment. We had to smile as we watched him.

"Orvar," said Jonathan. "Anyone can see from a long way that you're a prisoner from Katla Cavern."

It was true. All three of us were blood-stained and dirty, but Orvar looked the worst, his clothes in rags and his face scarcely visible what with his beard and hair. Only his eyes were visible, his strange, burning eyes.

There was a stream running through our crevice, so we rinsed all the dirt and blood off us there. I dipped my face into the cold water, again and again. It was wonderful; we felt that we were rinsing away the whole of Katla Cavern.

Then Orvar borrowed my knife and cut off a lot of his beard

and hair, so that he looked less like an escaped prisoner, and Jonathan took out of his pack the Tengil helmet and cloak that had got him out of Wild Rose Valley.

"Here, Orvar, put these on," he said. "Then perhaps they'll think you're a Tengilman who has taken two prisoners and you're on your way somewhere with them."

Orvar put on the helmet and cloak, but he didn't like them.

"This is the first and last time I'll ever put on such clothes," he said. "They reek of oppression and cruelty."

"Never mind what they reek of," said Jonathan, "as long as they help get you home to Wild Rose Valley."

The time had come now to leave. In an hour or two the sun would set and then it would be so dark in the mountains that no one would be able to find his way along those dangerous paths.

Jonathan looked very serious. He knew what we had to face and I heard him saying to Orvar:

"The next two hours will decide the fate of Wild Rose Valley, I think. Can you manage to ride for that long?"

"Yes, yes, yes," said Orvar. "For ten hours if you like."

He was to ride Fyalar. Jonathan helped him to mount, and at once he was quite a different Orvar, as if he were growing in the saddle and becoming strong. Yes, Orvar was one of those brave, strong people just like Jonathan. I was the only one who wasn't at all brave. But when we'd mounted and I was sitting there with my arms around Jonathan's waist and my forehead leaning against his back, it was as if a little of his strength came through to me and I was less afraid. And yet I couldn't help thinking how wonderful it'd be if we didn't always have to be strong and brave like this. If only we could be together again like during those first few days in Cherry Valley. Oh, how long ago it seemed now.

Then we set out on our journey. We rode toward the sunset,

for the bridge was in that direction. The paths were many and confusing in the mountains of Karmanyaka and no one but Jonathan could have found the right way in such a maze, but he managed in some strange way, fortunately for us.

I watched out for Tengilmen until my eyes ached, but none appeared, only Orvar riding behind us in his horrible helmet and black cloak. I felt a stab of fear every time I happened to turn my head and see him, so frightened had I become of those helmets and everyone who wore them.

We rode and rode and nothing happened. It was so calm and peaceful and beautiful all the way. A still evening in the mountains, you could call it, I thought. If only it hadn't been so untrue. Anything might appear in all that stillness and peacefulness, and all we felt was a kind of horrible excitement; even Jonathan was anxious and on his guard every moment.

"As long as we get to the bridge," he said, "then the worst will be over."

"How soon can we get there?" I asked.

"Within half an hour, if all goes well," said Jonathan.

But that was when we saw them, a troop of Tengilmen, six men with spears, on black horses, appearing where the path curved around a mountain wall, and trotting straight toward us.

"Now our lives are at stake," said Jonathan. "Move up, Orvar!"

Orvar rode quickly up beside us, and Jonathan flung his reins over to him, so that we should look a little more like prisoners.

They hadn't seen us yet, but it was too late to escape. There was nowhere to escape to, either. All we could do was to keep riding, hoping that Orvar's cloak and helmet would deceive them.

"I'll never give myself up alive," said Orvar. "I want you to know that, Lionheart."

152

As calmly as we could, we rode toward our enemies, getting nearer and nearer. Prickles were running down my spine, and I had time to think that if we were caught now, we might just as well have stayed in Katla Cavern and avoided the torment of a long night to no avail.

Then we met. They reined in their horses in order to pass us on the narrow path, and I saw that the leading rider was an old acquaintance, none other than Park.

But Park didn't look at us. He was looking at Orvar, and just as they passed each other, he said:

"Have you heard if they've found him yet?"

"No, I've heard nothing," said Orvar.

"Where are you going?" said Park.

"I've got a couple of prisoners," said Orvar. Park was given no more information and we rode on as fast as we dared.

"Turn around carefully, Rusky, and see what they're doing," said Jonathan, and I did as I was asked.

"They're riding away," I said.

"Thank goodness," said Jonathan.

But he had spoken too soon, for now I saw that they had stopped and were all looking back at us.

"They've begun to think," said Jonathan.

That was clearly what had happened.

"Stop a moment!" shouted Park. "Here, I want to take a closer look at you and your prisoners."

Orvar clenched his teeth.

"Ride on, Jonathan," he said. "Otherwise we're dead men."

And we rode on.

Then Park and the whole troop turned around; yes, they turned and came after us so fast that the manes of their horses were fluttering.

"Now, Grim, show them what you can do," said Jonathan.

153

And you too, my Fyalar, I thought, wishing that I myself was riding him.

No one had better steeds than Grim and Fyalar, who now flew along the path, knowing that it was a matter of life or death. Our pursuers were behind us; we heard their clattering hoofs, sometimes closer, sometimes farther away, but insistent; they did not go away, for now Park knew whom he was chasing, and no Tengilman could allow such a prey to get away. That would be a great prize to take back to Tengil in his castle.

With them at our heels we galloped over the bridge, and two spears came whistling after us, but they did not reach us.

Now we were over on the Nangiyala side and the worst should be over, Jonathan had said, but I couldn't see that that was so. The hunt was continued along the river. High up on the bank the bridle path leading into Wild Rose Valley twisted and turned, and we raced along it. This was the way we had come on another summer evening, which now seemed a thousand years ago, when we had come riding along at dusk, Jonathan and I, slowly riding on our way to our first campfire. That was how you should travel along rivers, not the way we were now, racing so that the horses almost fell.

Orvar rode the most wildly because he was riding home to Wild Rose Valley. Jonathan couldn't keep up with him, and Park was catching up on us; I couldn't think why until I realized it was because of me. There was no swifter rider than Jonathan, and no one would ever have been able to catch up with him if he had been alone on the horse, but now he had to think of me all the time and that hindered him.

This ride was to decide the fate of Wild Rose Valley, Jonathan had said. And I would be the one to decide how it would end. It would end badly; I became more and more sure of that. Every time I turned around to look, those black helmets were a little nearer, sometimes hidden behind a hillock or some trees, but then inexorably there again, nearer and nearer.

Jonathan knew as well as I did that we could not save our-selves now, not both of us, and it was necessary that Jonathan got away. I couldn't let him be captured because of me. So I said:

"Jonathan, do as I say now. Throw me off around a corner where they can't see. And catch up with Orvar!"

I saw that he was astonished at first, but not nearly so as-tonished as I was.

"Would you really dare?" said Jonathan.

"No, but I want to all the same," I said.

"Brave little Rusky," he said. "I'll come back and fetch you. As soon as I've left Orvar safe with Mathias, I'll come back."

"Promise?" I said.

"Yes, what do you think?" he said.

We had reached the willow tree where we had bathed, and I said:

"I'll hide in our tree. Fetch me from there."

I didn't have time to say more, for now we were hidden be-hind a hillock, and Jonathan reined in his horse so that I could slide down. Then he set off again and I rolled quickly aside into a hollow. I lay there listening to the soldiers thundering past. I saw Park's stupid face for one brief moment. He was snarling as if ready to bite—and Jonathan had saved the man's life!

But Jonathan had already caught up with Orvar. I saw them disappearing together and I was pleased. Ride on, old Park, I thought, if you think that helps. You'll see no more of Jonathan and Orvar.

I stayed in the hollow until Park and his men were also out of sight, then scrambled down to the river and my tree. It was good to crawl into the green center of the tree and settle into a forked branch, because I was tired now.

There was a little rowing boat bumping against the bank just by the tree. It must have torn itself loose from its moorings higher up the river, for it was not tied up. Whoever had lost it would be sad now, I thought, as I sat there looking around and wondering about this and that. I looked at the rushing water and Park's rock and thought that's where he should be sitting, that cowardly Park. And I saw Katla Mountain on the other side of the river and wondered how anybody could imprison other people in its terrible caves. I thought about Orvar and Jonathan and wished until it ached that they would escape into our underground passage before Park caught up with them. I wondered, too, what Mathias would say when he found Orvar in his hideout. How glad he would be. All that, I sat and thought about.

But dusk began to fall, and then I realized that I would perhaps have to spend the whole night there. Jonathan wouldn't have time to get back before dark. It was creepy, and anxiety began to crawl over me as dusk fell; I felt very lonely.

Then suddenly I saw a woman riding along high up on the riverbank, and it was none other than Sofia, yes, indeed, Sofia, and never had I been so pleased to see her as at that moment.

"Sofia!" I cried. "Sofia, here I am!"

I crawled out of the tree and waved my arms, but it was a long time before I could make her understand that it really was me.

"But, Karl," she called, "how did you get here? And where is Jonathan? Wait a minute, while we come down to you. We must water the horses, anyway."

Then I saw two men behind her, also mounted. I recognized one first—Hubert. The other man was hidden, but then he rode up and I saw him. It was Jossi.

156

But it *couldn't* be Jossi—I thought perhaps I had gone mad and was seeing things. Sofia couldn't have come here with Jossi! What had gone wrong? Was Sofia mad too, or had I just dreamt that Jossi was a traitor? No, no, I hadn't dreamt it; he was a traitor! I wasn't seeing things, here he was, and what would happen now?

He came riding down toward the river in the half-light and he called from a distance:

"Well, look who's here, little Karl Lionheart. Fancy meeting you again!"

All three of them came down, and I stood still waiting for them with only one thought in my head. Help, what will happen now?

They jumped down from their horses, and Sofia came running up to me and flung her arms around me, so glad that her eyes were shining.

"Are you out hunting wolves again?" said Hubert, laughing.

But I stood there without speaking, just staring.

"Where are you going?" I managed to get out at last.

"Jossi is going to show us where we can best get through the wall," said Sofia. "We must know to be ready when the battle actually starts."

"Yes, we must," said Jossi. "We must have a plan ready before we attack."

I was boiling inside. No doubt you've got your plan ready, I thought. I knew why he had come. He was going to lure Sofia and Hubert into a trap; straight to destruction, he would lure them, if no one stopped him. And then I understood: I am the one who must stop him, and it couldn't wait. It had to happen now. However much I disliked the idea, it had to happen now. But how should I begin?

"How's Bianca, Sofia?" I said at last.

Sofia looked sad.

"Bianca never came back from Wild Rose Valley," she said. "But do you know anything about Jonathan?"

She didn't want to talk about Bianca, but I had heard what I wanted to know; Bianca was dead. That was why Sofia had come here with Jossi. She had never received our message.

Jossi wanted to know, too, whether I knew anything about Jonathan.

"Surely he hasn't been captured?" he said.

"No, he hasn't," I said, and I looked straight into Jossi's eyes. "He's just rescued Orvar from Katla Cavern."

Jossi's red face turned pale and he fell silent. But Sofia and Hubert were delighted, so delighted that Sofia hugged me again and Hubert said:

"That's the best news you could have given us."

They wanted to know how it had all been done, but Jossi didn't, for now he was in a hurry.

"We can hear all about that later," he said. "We must go to where we're heading for now, before dark."

Yes, because Tengil's soldiers will no doubt be lying in wait, I thought.

"Come, Karl," said Sofia. "We can ride together on my horse, you and me."

"No," I said. "You mustn't ride anywhere with that traitor!"

I pointed at Jossi and I thought he would kill me. He grabbed hold of my neck with his great hands and snarled:

"What did you say? One more word and I'll finish you."

Sofia made him let me go, but she wasn't pleased with me.

"Karl, it's dreadful to call a person a traitor when it isn't true. But you're too young to know what you've just said."

Hubert just laughed quietly.

"I thought I was the traitor. I, who know so much and like

white horses, or whatever it was you wrote on the kitchen wall at home."

"Yes, Karl, you hurl your accusations in all directions," said Sofia sternly. "You must stop doing that."

"I'm sorry, Hubert," I said.

"Well, what about Jossi?" said Sofia.

"I won't say I'm sorry for calling a traitor a traitor," I said.

But I couldn't get them to believe me. It was dreadful when I realized that. They wanted to go on with Jossi. They were bringing their own misfortune on themselves, whatever I tried to do to stop them.

"He's leading you into a trap!" I cried. "I know he is. I know! Ask him about Veder and Kader, whom he meets up in the mountains. And ask him how he betrayed Orvar!"

Jossi looked as if he wanted to rush at me again, but he controlled himself.

"Can't we get going now," he said, "or are we to risk everything because of this boy's lies?"

He gave me a look full of hatred.

"And I liked you once," he said.

"I once liked you, too," I said.

I could see how scared he was beneath his rage. He really was in a hurry now, because he had to have Sofia captured and imprisoned before the truth dawned on her, otherwise his own life would be in question.

What a relief it must have been to him that Sofia didn't want to know the truth. She trusted Jossi and had always done so. And I, who had accused first one person and then another, how could she believe me?

"Come on now, Karl," she said. "I'll sort all this out with you later."

"There'll be no 'later' if you go with Jossi," I said.

I wept then. Nangiyala could not afford to lose Sofia, and here I was unable to save her, because she didn't want to be saved.

"Come on, Karl," she repeated obstinately.

But then I remembered something.

"Jossi," I said. "Open your shirt and show them what you've got on your chest."

Jossi turned so deathly pale that even Sofia and Hubert noticed it, and he put his hand on his chest as if wishing to protect something.

There was a brief silence, but then Hubert said in a harsh voice:

"Jossi, do as the boy says."

"We must hurry," he said, moving toward his horse.

Sofia's eyes hardened.

"Not so much hurry," she said. "I'm your leader, Jossi. Show me your chest."

It was terrible to see Jossi then, standing there panting, paralyzed, and afraid, not knowing whether to flee or stay. Sofia went up to him, but he thrust her aside with his elbow. He shouldn't have done that. She caught hold of him and tore open his shirt.

And there on his chest was the Katla mark: a dragon's head, glistening like blood.

Sofia turned even paler than Jossi.

"Traitor!" she said. "Curses on your head for what you have done to Nangiyala's valleys."

At last Jossi sprang into life. He swore and rushed over toward his horse, but Hubert was there before him. So he turned and looked around wildly for another escape route and caught sight of the rowing boat. With one single leap, he was into it and before Sofia or Hubert could even get to the bank, the current had carried him out of their reach.

160

Then he laughed, and it was a horrible laugh.

"I'll punish you, Sofia!" he cried. "When I come as chieftain of Cherry Valley, then I'll punish you."

You poor fool, you'll never get to Cherry Valley, I thought. You'll get to Karma Falls and nowhere else.

He tried to row, but raging waves and whirlpools caught the boat and tossed it between them, trying to crush it, tearing the oars from his hands, and then a hissing wave came and tipped him into the water. I wept then, wanting to save him, even though he was a traitor, but I knew there was no means of saving Jossi. It was so terrible and sad to stand there in the dusk, watching and knowing that Jossi was quite alone and helpless out there in the swirling waters. We saw him come up once on the crest of a wave, then he sank again and we saw no more of him.

It was almost dark now as the river of The Ancient Rivers took Jossi and carried him off to Karma Falls.

CHAPTER FIFTEEN

THE DAY OF THE BATTLE, THE DAY EVERYONE had been waiting for, came at last. There was a storm over Wild Rose Valley that day, so that trees were bent over and broken. But it wasn't that kind of storm Orvar had meant when he had said:

"The storm of liberation will come, and it will break the oppressors, as when a tree breaks and falls. It will go forward with a roar, sweeping away our slavery and finally freeing us again!"

He had spoken like that in Mathias's kitchen, to which people had come in secret to hear him and see him; yes, they wanted to see him and Jonathan.

"You two, you are our comfort and our hope, you are all we have," they said when they came creeping to Mathias's house in the evenings, although they knew how dangerous it was.

"Because they want to hear about the storm of liberation just as children want to hear sagas," said Mathias.

162

The day of the battle was the only thing they thought about or longed for now. This was not all that strange, for after Orvar's escape, Tengil had grown crueller than ever, every day finding new ways of tormenting and punishing Wild Rose Valley, which was why they hated him even more passionately than before and why even more weapons were being forged in the valley.

From Cherry Valley, more and more freedom fighters came to help. Sofia and Hubert had an army camp in the deepest depths of the forest, near Elfrida. Sofia sometimes came through the underground passage at night, and in Mathias's kitchen they made their battle plans, she and Orvar and Jonathan.

I lay there, listening to them, as I was sleeping on the sofa-bed in the kitchen, now that Orvar needed a place in the hideout. Every time Sofia came, she said:

"Here's my savior! I didn't forget to thank you, did I, Karl?"

Then Orvar said each time that I was the hero of Wild Rose Valley, but I could only think about Jossi out in the dark waters and feel sad.

Sofia also arranged for a supply of bread for Wild Rose Valley. It was brought over the mountains from Cherry Valley in wagons and was smuggled through the underground passage. Mathias went around with a pack on his back and in secret shared it out among the houses. I hadn't known before that people could be made so happy with nothing but a little bit of bread. Now I saw it, because I went with Mathias on his walks, and I saw how the people in the valley were suffering and I heard them talk about the battle they were longing for so much.

I was frightened of that day, and yet I almost began to long for it in the end, I too, for it was unbearable to go on waiting, and dangerous, Jonathan said.

"You can't keep so much so secret for so long," he said to

163

Orvar. "Our dream of liberation could be crushed so easily."

He was certainly right in that. It needed only one Tengil-man to find that underground passage, or a renewed search of houses, for Jonathan and Orvar to be discovered in the hideout. I shuddered at the very thought of it.

But the Tengilmen must have been both blind and deaf, or they would surely have noticed *something*. If they had listened just a little, they would have been able to hear how that storm of liberation was beginning to rumble, the storm that was soon going to shake the whole of Wild Rose Valley. But they didn't.

The night before the day of the battle, I was lying in my sofa-bed, unable to sleep because of the storm outside and because of my own anxiety. It had been decided that the battle would start at dawn the next morning. Orvar and Jonathan and Mathias were sitting at the table talking about it, and I was lying there listening. Orvar spoke the most; he talked and talked, his eyes glowing. He was longing for the morning more than anyone else.

This was how it was to go, as far as I could make out from their talk. The guards at the main gateway and the river gateway were to be struck down first, so that the gates could be opened for Sofia and Hubert, who would then ride in with their forces, Sofia through the main gateway, Hubert through the river gateway.

"And then we must be victorious together or die," said Orvar.

It must go quickly, he said. The valley must be freed of all Tengilmen and the gateways closed again before Tengil had time to bring Katla, for there were no weapons against Katla. She could not be defeated in any other way except by starvation, Orvar said.

"Neither spears nor arrows nor swords affect her," he said.

"And one tiny little lick of her fire is enough to paralyze or kill anyone."

"But if Tengil has Katla over there in his mountains, what's the use of liberating Wild Rose Valley?" I said. "With her, he can suppress you again, just as he did the first time."

"He has given us a wall to protect us, don't forget that," said Orvar. "And gateways that can be shut against monsters. Kind man that he is."

I need no longer worry about Tengil, Orvar said, for in the evening he and Jonathan, Sofia and some others were to penetrate into Tengil's castle, overwhelm his guard and finish him off there, before he was even aware of the rebellion in the valley. Then Katla would be chained up in her cave until she grew so weak and starved that they could kill her.

"There's no other way of getting rid of such a monster," said Orvar.

Then he again spoke of how swiftly they must rid the valley of all Tengilmen, and Jonathan said:

"Rid? You mean kill?"

"Yes, what else would I mean?" said Orvar.

"But I can't kill anyone," said Jonathan. "You know that, Orvar."

"Not even if it's a question of your own life?" said Orvar.

"No, not even then," said Jonathan.

Orvar couldn't understand that, and neither could Mathias.

"If everyone were like you," said Orvar, "then evil would reign forever."

But then I said that if everyone were like Jonathan, there wouldn't be any evil.

Then I didn't say anything else for the rest of the evening, except when Mathias came and tucked me in. Then I whispered to him:

"I'm frightened, Mathias."

Mathias patted me and said:

"So am I."

All the same Jonathan had to promise Orvar that he would ride around in the confusion of battle to give other people the courage to do what he himself could not or would not do.

"The people of Wild Rose Valley must see you," said Orvar. "They must see both of us."

Then Jonathan said:

"Well, if I must, I must."

But I saw how pale he was in the light of the one little candle in the kitchen.

We had had to leave Grim and Fyalar in the forest with Elfrida, when we had come back from Katla Cavern. But it had been decided that Sofia was to bring them with her when she rode through the main gate on the day of the battle.

What I was to do had also been decided. I was to do nothing, only wait until it was all over. Jonathan had said that. I was to sit all alone at home in the kitchen and wait.

No one slept much that night.

Then the morning came.

Yes, then the morning came and, with it, the day of the battle. Oh, how sick at heart I was that day! I saw and heard more than enough of blood and cries, for they were fighting on the slopes below Mathias's house. I saw Jonathan riding around, the storm tearing at his hair, and all about him nothing but fighting and flashing swords and whistling spears and flying arrows and cries and cries; and I said to Fyalar, if Jonathan dies, then I want to die too.

Yes, Fyalar was with me in the kitchen. I had thought of not telling anyone about it, but I had to have him there. I *couldn't*

166

be alone, I just couldn't. Fyalar also looked out of the window at what was happening on the slopes below. Then he whinnied. I didn't know whether that was because he wished to join Grim or whether he was as frightened as I was.

I was frightened, frightened, frightened.

I saw Veder fall to Sofia's spear and Kader die by Orvar's sword, Dodik too, and several more, falling right and left, and Jonathan riding there in the middle of it all, the storm tearing at his hair, his face growing paler and paler, and my heart grew more and more sick within me.

And then the end came!

Many cries were heard in Wild Rose Valley that day, but one came that was like no other.

In the middle of the battle, a battlehorn sounded through the storm and a cry went up:

"Katla's coming!"

Then came the scream, Katla's scream of hunger, which everyone knew so well. Swords and spears and arrows fell to the ground and they who were fighting could fight no more, for they knew there was no saving them now. Nothing but the thunder of the storm and Tengil's battlehorn and Katla's screams could be heard in the valley, and then Katla's fire hissed out, killing everyone whom Tengil pointed at. He pointed and pointed, and his cruel face was dark with evil; now I knew that the end of Wild Rose Valley had come.

I didn't want to look, I didn't want to look—at anything. Except Jonathan. I had to know where he was, and I saw him just below Mathias's house, sitting there on Grim, pale and still, the storm tearing at his hair.

"Jonathan," I cried. "Jonathan, can you hear me?"

But he didn't hear me and I saw him spur on his horse and fly down the slope like an arrow, flying faster than anyone in heaven or on earth had ever flown, I know. He was flying toward Tengil . . . and he flew past him . . .

Then the battlehorn sounded again, but it was Jonathan who was blowing it now. He had snatched it out of Tengil's hand and was blowing it so that it resounded, so that Katla should know that she had a new master.

Then it was quite quiet, even the storm dying down. Everyone fell silent, just waiting. Tengil was sitting taut with fear on his horse, waiting. Katla was waiting, too.

Once again Jonathan blew on the horn.

Then Katla screamed and turned in rage on the man she had once obeyed so blindly.

"Tengil's time will come one day," Jonathan had said, I remembered.

It had come now.

That was the end of the day of battle in Wild Rose Valley. Many people had given their lives for the sake of freedom. Yes, their valley was free now, but the dead were lying there and did not know it.

Mathias was dead and I no longer had a grandfather. Hubert was dead, the first to fall. He had never even got through the river gateway, because there he had met Tengil and his soldiers; and worst of all, he had met Katla. Tengil had brought her with him that very day to punish Wild Rose Valley for the last time for Orvar's escape. He had not known it was the day of battle, though when he realized it, no doubt he had been glad Katla was with him.

But he was dead now, Tengil, just as dead as the others.

"Our tormentor is no more," said Orvar. "Our children will be able to live in freedom and be happy. Soon Wild Rose Valley will be as before."

But I thought that Wild Rose Valley would never be the same as before, not for me, without Mathias.

Orvar had received a sword wound in his back, but it was as if he didn't feel it or didn't mind about it. His eyes were just as glowing as he spoke to the people in the valley.

"We shall be happy again," he said, over and over again.

There were many people who wept that day in Wild Rose Valley. But not Orvar.

Sofia was alive, not even wounded, and was now to return to Cherry Valley, she and all her surviving warriors.

She came to us to say farewell outside Mathias's house.

"This was where Mathias lived," she said, weeping a little. Then she embraced Jonathan.

"Come home to Knights Farm soon," she said. "I'll think of you every moment until we meet again."

Then she looked at me.

"Karl, are you coming with me?"

"No," I said. "No, I shall go with Jonathan."

I was afraid that Jonathan would send me away with Sofia but he didn't. "I'd like to have Karl with me," he said.

On the slope below Mathias's house, Katla was lying like a horrible great lump, silent and satiated with blood. Now and again she looked at Jonathan, like a dog looking to find out what his master wants. She touched no one now, but as long as she was lying there, terror lay over the valley and no one dared be happy. Wild Rose Valley could neither celebrate its freedom nor grieve for its dead as long as Katla existed, Orvar said. The only person who could get her back to her cave was Jona-than.

"Will you help Wild Rose Valley just once more," said Orvar. "If you take her there and chain her up, then I'll do the rest when the time is ripe."

"Yes," said Jonathan. "I will help you one last time, Orvar."

I know how you should travel along rivers. You should ride slowly and watch the river flowing down there, the water glittering and the branches of willow trees dancing in the wind. You shouldn't travel there with a dragon at your heels.

But that's what we did, listening to the heavy tramp of her feet behind us. Thump, thump, thump, thump: she sounded so alarming as she walked that Grim and Fyalar almost went mad. We could hardly hold them. Now and again Jonathan blew the horn, but that was a horrible sound too, and Katla certainly didn't like it. But she had to obey when she heard it. That was the only thing that comforted me on our ride.

We did not say a word to each other, Jonathan and I; we just rode as hard as we could. Jonathan had to chain Katla up in her cave before night and darkness fell, and there she would die. Then we would never see her again and we would forget that there was such a country as Karmanyaka. The mountains of The Ancient Mountains could stand there for all eternity, but we would never travel that way again, Jonathan had promised me.

It grew still toward evening, no longer stormy, but a calm, warm evening, and it was beautiful when the sun had set, just the kind of evening in which you should ride along rivers without being afraid, I thought.

But I didn't let Jonathan see it, that I was afraid, I mean.

At last we reached Karma Falls.

"Karmanyaka, here we are for the last time," said Jonathan as we rode across the bridge. Then he blew the horn.

Katla saw her cliff on the other side of the river. She clearly wanted to get there, because an eager hissing came from her, right at Grim's hocks. She shouldn't have done that.

For then it happened. Grim shied away in terror against the bridge rail, and I screamed because I thought Jonathan was going to go headlong into Karma Falls. He didn't, but the horn

171

flew out of his hand and vanished into the rushing water below.

Katla's cruel eyes had seen it all, and now she knew she no longer had a master. Then she screamed, and fire began to stream out of her nostrils.

Oh, how we rode to save our wretched lives! How we rode, how we rode! Over the bridge and up the path toward Tengil's castle, with Katla hissing after us.

That path, it zigzagged its way up through the mountain of The Ancient Mountains, and not even in a dream could anything have been so terrible as fleeing from ledge to ledge with Katla after you, her fire almost licking the horses' hocks. A flame shot horribly close to Jonathan, and for one terrible moment I thought he'd been burned, but he cried:

"Don't stop. Ride on, ride on!"

Poor Grim and Fyalar, Katla harried them so that they almost burst trying to get away from her. Up the path they raced, through twists and turns, the lather spattering from them, racing faster and faster until they could do no more. But by then Katla had fallen behind too, and was screaming with rage. She was on her own ground now and no one was going to get away from there. Her thump, thump, thump, increased its pace and I knew she would win in the end, in all her stubborn cruelty.

We went on riding for a long, long time like that, and I had given up all hope of rescue.

We had come quite a way up the mountain now and were still ahead. We could see Katla immediately below us on a narrow rock ledge above Karma Falls. She stopped there for a while, for this was her cliff. It was here she used to stand and stare, and that's what she did now, too. Almost reluctantly she stopped and stared down into the waterfall, fire and smoke pouring from her nostrils as she tramped impatiently back and forth. But then she remembered us and glared up at us with her smoldering eyes.

172

You cruel thing, I thought. You cruel, cruel thing, why don't you stay there on your ledge?

But I knew she would come. She would come . . .

We had reached the great rock where we had seen her thrusting out her terrible head the first time we had ever come to Karmanyaka. Suddenly our horses could go no farther. It is horrible when your horse collapses beneath you, but that was what happened. Grim and Fyalar just sank down onto the path, and if we had previously hoped for a miracle to save us, now there was nothing left but to give up hope.

We were lost, we knew. And Katla knew it too, a look of devilish triumph coming into her eyes. She stood quite still on her ledge and glared up at us. I thought she was laughing mockingly at us. She was in no hurry now. It was as if she were thinking: I'll come in good time. You can expect me, don't worry.

Jonathan looked at me in that kind way of his.

"Forgive me, Rusky, for dropping the horn," he said. "But I couldn't help it."

I wanted to tell Jonathan that I had never, never, had anything to forgive him for, but I was struck dumb with terror.

Katla stayed down there, fire and smoke coming out in spurts from her nostrils, her feet beginning to tramp. We were sheltering behind the great rock so that her flames could not reach us. I was holding on to Jonathan hard; oh, how hard I held on, and he looked at me with tears in his eyes.

Then a great rage came over him and he leaned forward and shouted at Katla down there:

"You may not touch Rusky! Do you hear, you monster, you! You may not touch, Rusky, or else. . . ."

He grasped the rock as if he were a giant and could frighten her. He was no giant and could not frighten Katla, but the rock was lying loose on the edge of the precipice.

"Neither spears nor arrows nor swords affect Katla," Orvar

had said. He might also have said that neither do rocks, however large the rock is.

Katla wasn't killed by the rock which Jonathan tipped onto her, but it fell straight on her, and with a scream which would demolish mountains, she fell backward into Karma Falls.

CHAPTER SIXTEEN

NO, JONATHAN DIDN'T KILL KATLA. KARM DID. And Katla killed Karm. In front of our very eyes. We saw it. No one else but Jonathan and I had seen two monsters from ancient times destroy each other. We saw them fight to their deaths in Karma Falls.

When Katla let out that scream and disappeared, at first we could not believe it. It was impossible to believe that she was really gone. Where she had sunk, we saw nothing but whirling foam. Nothing more. No Katla.

But then we saw the serpent. He raised his green head out of the foam and his tail whipped up the water. Oh, he was terrible, a giant serpent, as long as the river is wide, just as Elfrida had said.

The sea serpent of Karma Falls that she had heard sagas about when she was small was no more a saga than Katla. He existed and was a monster as horrible as Katla herself, his head swaying in all directions, searching . . . and then he saw Katla. She

175

floated up out of the depths and was suddenly in the middle of the whirlpools, and the serpent threw himself headlong at her and coiled himself around her. She spurted her death-dealing fire at him, but he squeezed her so hard that the fire went out in her breast. Then she snapped at him and he snapped back. They snapped and bit, both of them wanting to kill. I suppose they had longed for this since ancient times. Yes, they snapped and bit like two raging creatures, hurling their terrible bodies at each other in the swirling water, Katla screaming between bites, Karm snapping quite silently, black dragon blood and green serpent blood floating out into the white foam, coloring it dark and sickly.

How long did it go on? It seemed to me as if I had stood there on that path for a thousand years and had never seen anything else but those two raging monsters in their ultimate battle.

It was a long and terrible battle, but it came to an end at last. A piercing shriek came from Katla, her death cry, and then she was silent. Karm had no head left by then, but his body did not let her go and they sank together, closely intertwined, down into the depths. And then there was no Katla and no Karm; they were gone as if they had never existed. The foam was white again, and the poisonous monster blood was rinsed away by the mighty waters of Karma Falls. Everything was as before, as it had been since ancient times.

We stood gasping there on the path, although it was all over. We could not speak for a long while, but at last Jonathan said:

"We must leave! Quickly! It'll be dark soon and I don't want night to fall on us in Karmanyaka."

Poor Grim and Fyalar. I don't know how we got them to their feet or how we got away. They were so tired they could hardly lift their legs.

But we left Karmanyaka and rode for the last time across the bridge. Then the horses could not take another step. As soon

176

as we reached the other side of the bridge, they sank down and just lay there, as if they were thinking, now that we've helped you into Nangiyala, that'll have to do.

"We'll make a campfire at our old place," said Jonathan, meaning the cliff where we had been during the thunderstorm night, when I had seen Katla for the first time. I still shuddered when I thought about it, and I would have preferred to camp elsewhere. But we couldn't go on any farther now.

The horses had to be watered first before we could settle down for the night. We gave them some, but they didn't want to drink. They were too tired. I was worried.

"Jonathan, there's something peculiar about them," I said. "Do you think they'll be better after some sleep?"

"Yes, everything will be better when they've had some sleep," said Jonathan.

I patted Fyalar, who was lying with his eyes closed.

"What a day you've had, poor Fyalar," I said. "But tomorrow, everything will be all right, Jonathan says."

We built a fire on exactly the same place where we had made our first one, and the thunderstorm cliff was indeed the best place you could think of for a campfire, if only you could forget that Karmanyaka was so near. Behind us there were high mountain walls, still warm from the sun, and shelter from all winds. In front of us, the precipice fell straight down into Karma Falls, and the side nearest the bridge was also a steep slope down toward a green meadow, which from here looked like a tiny green speck, far, far below.

We sat by our fire and watched dusk fall over the mountains of The Ancient Mountains and the river of The Ancient Rivers. I was tired and thought that I had never lived through such a long hard day in my life. From dawn to dusk, there had been nothing but blood and fear and death. There are adventures that shouldn't happen, Jonathan had once said, and we had had more than enough of that kind that day. The day of the battle—it had indeed been long and hard, but now it was over at last.

Yet our grief had not ended. I thought about Mathias. I grieved for him very much, and as we sat by the fire, I asked Jonathan:

"Where do you think Mathias is now?"

"He's in Nangilima," said Jonathan.

"Nangilima, I've never heard of that," I said.

"Yes, you have," said Jonathan. "Don't you remember that morning when I left Cherry Valley and you were so afraid? Don't you remember what I said then? 'If I don't come back, we'll meet in Nangilima.' That's where Mathias is now."

Then he told me about Nangilima. He hadn't told me stories for a long time because we had had no time. But now as he sat by the fire and talked about Nangilima, it was almost as if he were sitting on the edge of my sofa-bed at home in town.

"In Nangilima . . . in Nangilima," said Jonathan in that voice he always used when he was telling stories. "It's still in the days of campfires and sagas there."

"Poor Mathias, so there are adventures there that shouldn't happen," I said.

But Jonathan said that Nangilima was not in the days of cruel sagas but in days that were happy and full of games. The people played there; they worked, too, of course, and helped each other with everything, but they played a lot and sang and danced and told stories, he said. Sometimes they scared the children with terribly cruel sagas about monsters like Karm and Katla, and about cruel men like Tengil. But afterward they laughed.

"Were you afraid, then?" they said to the children. "They're only sagas. Things that have never existed. Not here in our valleys, at least."

Mathias was happy in Nangilima, Jonathan said. He had an old farm in Apple Valley, the most beautiful farm in the loveliest and greenest of Nangilima's valleys.

"Soon it'll be time to pick the apples in his orchard," said Jonathan. "Then we should be there to help him. He's too old to climb ladders."

"I almost wish we could go there," I said. I thought it sounded so pleasant in Nangilima and I longed to see Mathias again.

"Do you think so?" said Jonathan. "Well, we could live with Mathias. At Mathias Farm in Apple Valley in Nangilima."

"Tell me what it would be like," I said.

"Oh, it'd be fine," said Jonathan. "We could ride around in the forests and build campfires here and there—if only you knew what the forests around the Nangilima valleys were like! And deep in the forests lie small clear lakes. We could build a campfire by a different lake every evening and be away for days and nights and then go back home to Mathias again."

"And help him with the apples," I said. "But then Sofia and Orvar would have to look after Cherry Valley and Wild Rose Valley without you, Jonathan."

"Well, why not?" said Jonathan. "Sofia and Orvar don't need me any longer. They can put things right for themselves in their valleys."

But then he fell silent and told no more stories. We were silent, both of us, and I was tired and not at all happy. It was no comfort to hear about Nangilima, which was so far away from us.

Dusk grew deeper and deeper and the mountains blacker and blacker. Great black birds swayed above us and cried so dismally that everything seemed desolate. Karma Falls was thundering away and I was tired of hearing it. It made me remember what I wanted to forget. Sad, sad, everything was, and I'll never be happy again, I thought.

I moved nearer to Jonathan. He was sitting very still, leaning against the mountain wall, and his face was pale. He looked like a prince in a saga as he sat there, but a pale and exhausted prince. Poor Jonathan, you're not happy either, I thought. Oh, if only I could make you a little happy.

As we were sitting there in silence, Jonathan suddenly said: "Rusky, there's something I must tell you."

I was afraid at once, because when he said that, it was always something sad he had to tell.

"What must you tell me?" I said.

He stroked my cheek with his forefinger.

"Don't be afraid, Rusky . . . but do you remember what Orvar said? A tiny lick of Katla's fire is enough to paralyze or kill anyone—do you remember him saying that?"

"Yes, but why talk about that now?" I said.

"Because . . ." said Jonathan. "Because a little flame of Katla's fire touched me as we were fleeing from her."

My heart had been sick all day with sorrow and fear, but I hadn't wept. Now tears came from me almost like a cry.

"Are you going to die again, Jonathan?" I cried. And Jonathan said:

"No. But that's what I'd like to do. Because I'll never be able to move again."

He explained the cruelty of Katla's fire to me. If it didn't kill, it did something that was much worse. It destroyed something inside so that you were paralyzed. You did not notice at first, but it crept up on you, slowly and inexorably.

"I can move only my arms now," he said. "And soon I won't be able to do that."

"But don't you think it'll pass?" I said, weeping.

"No, Rusky, it'll never pass," said Jonathan. "Unless I can get to Nangilima."

Unless he could get to Nangilima. Oh, now I understood! He

was thinking of leaving me alone again, I knew it! Once he had vanished to Nangiyala without me . . .

"But not again," I cried. "Not without me! You mustn't vanish to Nangilima without me!"

"Do you want to come with me, then?" he asked.

"Yes, what do you think?" I said. "Haven't I told you that wherever you go, I'll go too?"

"You've said that, and it's a comfort to me," said Jonathan. "But it's difficult to get there."

He sat silently for a while, and then he said:

"Do you remember that time when we jumped? That terrible time during the fire and we jumped down into the yard? I went to Nangiyala then, do you remember?"

"Of course I remember," I said, weeping even more. "How can you ask? Do you think I haven't remembered it every single moment since?"

"Yes, I know," said Jonathan, stroking my cheek again.

And then he said:

"I thought perhaps we could jump again. Down the precipice here—down onto the meadow."

"Well, then we'll die," I said. "But would we come to Nangilima then?"

"Yes, you can be sure of that," said Jonathan. "As soon as we land we'll see the light from Nangilima. We'll see the morning light over Nangilima's valleys, because it's morning there now."

"Ha-ha, we can jump straight into Nangilima," I said, and I laughed for the first time in a long time.

"Yes, we can," said Jonathan. "And as soon as we land, we'll see the path to Apple Valley, too, right in front of us. And Grim and Fyalar are already there waiting for us. We would only have to mount and ride away."

"And you wouldn't be paralyzed then?" I said.

"No, I'll be free of all evil and as happy as anything. And

you too, Rusky, you'll be happy too. The path to Apple Valley goes through the forest. What do you think it'll feel like, riding there in the morning sun, you and I?"

"Good," I said, and laughed again.

"And we'll be in no hurry," said Jonathan. "We can bathe in some small lake, if we want to. We'd still get to Mathias's before he has the soup ready."

"How glad he'll be that we've come," I said. But then I felt as if I had received a blow from a club. Grim and Fyalar—how could Jonathan think that we could take them with us to Nangilima?

"How can you say that they're already there waiting for us? They're lying asleep over there."

"They are not sleeping, Rusky. They're dead. From Katla's fire. But what you see over there is only their shells. Believe me, Grim and Fyalar are already down on the path to Nangilima, waiting for us."

"Let's hurry then," I said, "so that they don't have to wait too long."

Then Jonathan looked at me and smiled slightly.

"I can't hurry at all," he said. "I can't move from the spot, don't forget."

And then I realized what I had to do.

"Jonathan, I'll take you on my back," I said. "You did that for me once. And now I'll do it for you. That's only fair."

"Yes, that's fair," said Jonathan. "But do you think you dare, Rusky Lionheart?"

I went over to the precipice and looked down. It was already too dark and I could hardly see the meadow. But it was so far down that it made you gasp. If we jumped down there, then at least we'd be sure of getting to Nangilima, both of us. No one need stay behind alone and lie grieving and weeping and being afraid.

But it was not *we* who had to jump. It was *I* who was to do it. It was difficult to get to Nangilima, Jonathan had said, and now I knew why. How would I dare, how could I ever dare?

Well, if you don't dare now, I thought, then you're a little bit of filth and you'll never be anything else but a little bit of filth.

I went back to Jonathan.

"Yes, I dare," I said.

"Brave little Rusky," he said. "Let's do it then."

"I want to sit here for a while with you first," I said.

"Not too long," said Jonathan.

"No, only until it's quite dark," I said. "So that I see nothing."

And I sat beside him and held his hand and felt that he was strong and good through and through and that nothing was really dangerous so long as he was there.

Then night and darkness fell over Nangiyala, over mountains and river and land, and I stood by the precipice with Jonathan holding on to me hard with his arms around my neck, and I felt how he was breathing on my ear from behind. He was breathing quite calmly. Not like me—Jonathan, my brother, why am I not so brave as you?

I couldn't see the precipice below me, but I knew that it was there, and I needed to take only one step out into the dark and it would all be over. It would go so quickly.

"Rusky Lionheart," said Jonathan. "Are you afraid?"

"No—yes, I'm afraid. But I'll do it all the same, Jonathan, I'm doing it now—now—and then I'll never be afraid again. Never again be afr—"

"Oh, Nangilima! Yes, Jonathan, yes, I can see the light! *I can see the light!*"

ABOUT THE AUTHOR

Astrid Lindgren is one of the most popular writers of children's books, best known for her novels about Pippi Longstocking, whose adventures have been translated into every major language. Mrs. Lindgren is one of the twelve most translated authors in the world, and the most widely read writer in her native Sweden.

Mrs. Lindgren has received many awards and honors in recognition of her contribution to children's literature, including the Hans Christian Andersen Medal, and the "litteris et artibus" presented to her by the King of Sweden for her literary achievements. She is also the first children's author ever to receive the Swedish State Award.

Astrid Lindgren was born on a farm in the village of Smaland in Sweden. The happy childhood she lived there has provided much of the inspiration for her books, as have her two children, for whom she wrote the *Pippi Longstocking* books. In addition to her work as an author, she has worked as a journalist and an editor of children's books. She now lives in Stockholm, Sweden.